a ...nks so much for
allowing me to share my story
with you!

are amazing.

Advance Praise for *WHO R U?*

"Sit down, grab the tissues, and get ready for a rollercoaster ride of emotions. The battles Angelia Robinson has fought are traumatizing in so many ways. Her story shifts from anger to joy and sadness to triumph, reminding us throughout that our past need not define our future. Be prepared to pick your jaw up off the floor quite a few times. I know I did!"

-Leann Rhodes, Author
"Rise Up Shine On" and "Just Prevail:
In The Middle Of The Storm"

"Reading this book was so liberating. It made me feel that I was not alone on this journey called life, and all the good, bad, and ugly that comes with it. It is such a relatable story that it had me crying, laughing, and celebrating right along with Angelia. She is full of light, grace, and compassion. Her book is a must read."

-Cynthia Cosby, Owner
Clover Creations, LLC

"This book gave me chills. I laughed, I cried, and I was able to relate to everything Angelia suffered. The tales in here are all very relatable, opening up wounds in me that I thought had healed."

-Ameisha Gathers, Entrepreneur

"*Who R U?* is a fascinating window into a chaotic world I knew nothing about. Angelia Robinson has led an unbelievable life. I couldn't put her book down."

-Jill Holden, Actress and Educator

"*Who R U?* is not just the autobiography of Angelia Robinson but a look into the soul of women who suffer in silence. It is a book that any woman can relate to. I had the same uncle whose lap I could not sit in because of his perverted ways. I too know women who punish their children for the sins of the father. The author's transparency will help so many women who have been through hell understand that their story is not over. In fact, it's only just begun."

-ReShan Adams, Intimacy Coach

"By the end of Chapter 1, I was already breathing hard, like I was running alongside Angelia. Her book left me on the edge of my seat. It's an amazing read."

-Donna F. Durante Miller,
Authoress and Distiller

WHO R U?

Tales of a Survivor

Angelia Robinson

Angelia can be contacted at whorubio@gmail.com

Publishing Company: Who R U Publishing

ISBN: 978-1-7364591-0-2 (hardcover)
ISBN: 978-1-7364591-1-9 (ebook)

Interior Page Design: Mary Neighbour

Cover Design (front/back): Hakim Taylor
and Gregory Taylor

Cover Photo Credit (front/back): Darnell Porter

AUTHOR'S NOTE

This book materialized from the moments I've lived, which molded me into the evolved woman I am today. I have miraculously not only been able to survive into almost middle age but, by the grace of God, I've successfully protected my inner light, that gift that has made my journey all the more meaningful. Fear and rejection have given way to courage and strength. Darkness and pain have transformed into love.

Please note that every effort was taken in the following pages to produce truthfulness and accuracy in the retelling. Some of the names have been changed, and individuals in my life were assigned pseudonyms to protect their privacy. However, this should in no way be construed as an alteration or watering down of the facts, which are consistent to my own recollection.

As you read my story, may you reflect on your own tales and, hopefully, relate in some way to the bumpy ride that finally dropped me in a place of peace and emotional freedom.

To all the women who have survived abuse and trauma, this book is for you. My name may be on it, but it's also your story.

TOGETHER we can survive anything! Empowerment is the name of the game!

Contents

PREFACE

Everyone has a story to tell. That's one thing I've learned in my 48 years on this planet. But I may be unusual in that I seem to have far more stories than your average human, making the need for me to get them all down in a book less a labor of love than of necessity.

As I was telling my girlfriend the other day, "Man, I've lived so many different lives. I've been everyone from the in-the-hood chick to the suburban girl to the drug kingpin's wife to everything in-between." I realize that probably makes me more relatable, having gone through so many things others have experienced as well.

That's one of the primary reasons I wanted to write this book. I thought it could prove entertaining and enlightening to a wide variety of people. I also feel like my experiences may be informative for people and help them to avoid some of the mistakes I've made. I would love to hear somebody say, "Ooh, when I read that in your book, it changed my life. Thank you."

Helping people fuels me. It's my energy source. One way I feel like I can help them right off the top is to assure them that no matter where they are in their lives, *it's never too late to be who or what you might have been.* That's basically a mantra for me. I hope people who are reading this can take those words to heart and really believe them.

I want to assure you right here and right now—before you go any further—that I've never thought of myself as this pillar of wisdom. Far from it, in fact. I'm the girl who made endless mistakes, who always found herself looking for love in all the wrong places. There are so many women who share my story about that basic need to be loved and validated. In that process, many of us are mishandled, misused and abused. That's especially true if you have mommy and daddy issues. (Yeah, me too.)

People are often poisoned early in their lives, whether it's the environment they're in, the things they see, or the things that were done to them (and perhaps are doomed to repeat). On paper, it seems they don't have a chance. Yet that doesn't mean they'll never have an opportunity to come out of it and emerge a good person or, at the least, a productive member of society. Isn't that what's expected of us, anyway?

Where are the stories for the girls like me? Women my age are still sometimes little girls inside, because they never healed from what they suffered at an early age. That desperate search for answers and healing continues throughout their lifetime. It's the reason that women too often settle for the guy who treats them like crap and reject the nice guy. They're used to the physical or emotional abuse. That's their comfort zone. It's really like any other addiction.

Not everybody has that special person who can speak to their spirit or their soul and help them to get out of the cycle of accepting being treated like garbage. By sharing our stories, we can heal. Knowledge PUT TO USE is power, and so is telling people who we are and where we've been. People need other people they can relate to, so they don't feel like they're the only ones who are fucked up. Trust me, we're *all* fucked up in one way or another. But that's okay. It's how we turn that fuck-up into a come-up that matters.

Too many of us live in this fantasy where we like to portray to the world what I like to call "our representative." They just love to give this impression of, "Oh, my life is so great!"—and it makes it look like everything is beautiful when they're really dying on the inside. A false sense of reality is what fuels social media too. Social media is killing what's left of humanity.

The book you're about to read is the opposite of that. I'm not pretending to be anything close to perfect, trust me. In fact, I'm writing this book *scared*. I just want to show people that you can face a huge amount of adversity and come out on the other side bigger *and* stronger. I've long been very musical and have reached a lot of people that way, but not as many as I could have or should have—or hopefully that I can.

What else? Well, I'm hardheaded and stubborn, a free spirit who wants to do things her way or no way. I also know that the abuse and trauma I suffered early in my life still impacts me today. It's made me super aggressive, for one thing. I'm an alpha female in my work life, in my social life, and in the bedroom. I refuse to be controlled. Thank God it never resulted in drug or alcohol addiction, but it's a part of me that I'm learning to manage daily, as if I were in some sort of a recovery program.

But I've also got to say that today, I'm happier than I've ever been in my life. Instead of worrying about what tomorrow is going to bring, I look forward to every step I'm taking on this journey. I feel like Superwoman! I now see myself traveling the world, speaking to millions and inspiring them to become the best version of themselves. Being out there with the people is what it's about for me, especially with the women. Being confined to a desk is like kryptonite to me. I refuse to go back there, and I see it as my mission to encourage you, in the words of the great Maya Angelou, to "pursue the things you love doing and then do them so well that people can't take their eyes off of you."

If someone like me can write an autobiography that makes you smile, laugh, cry, or cringe, and at the same time makes you think about or change what you might do in a similar situation, then anyone can.

Thanks for taking this ride with me!

1 TRAUMA

TRAUMA IS SOMETHING THAT EVERYONE will experience at some point in their lives. For some, it happens as early as in the womb; for others, they may go through it shortly after birth and then again many times throughout their entire lives. As I begin to tell you about my own, I am currently living in the midst of traumas that are taking over our world. The death of Kobe Bryant, the BLACK LIVES MATTER movement, COVID-19, and one of the biggest and most important elections of our time. It's been scary, to say the least.

Death has never been my friend, and to see it happening all around me can at times be paralyzing and super depressing. See, depression just doesn't work for me. It's another form of kryptonite. I'm Superwoman in my mind, and all this political BS and racial tension have tried to paralyze me. I can't have that, because I have so much more to give.

But take a minute to travel with me back in time.

It was 1976.

I was four.

This is my earliest memory. My friends and I were playing around in the neighborhood, being mischievous like most kids are. I don't know why I did it. Why did I decide to grab that maintenance man's mop and hide it from him? It was stupid, innocent fun that would end up changing the course of my life forever. He was so angry that we were taunting him, and so I suggested that we run and hide in one of the nearby apartment buildings.

"Damn, what do we do?" I asked my best friend, Lajuan Womack.

"Run!" she said.

So, we ran. Man, did we run. We had to get away from that mean, old maintenance man. I was afraid he might really hurt us for teasing him.

"Hey," I said to Lajuan, pointing at a nearby building, "let's hide there."

"Do we know anyone in there?"

I thought for a minute. "Yeah," I said. "There's that guy who's so nice and gives us candy all the time."

"Good," Lajuan said, "let's go!"

What a BIG mistake I was making. Little did I know that this would be the first of many, many times that I would be the victim of sexual assault. Now remember, I am four years old here. It's hard to believe, right? Hell, I don't even know why we were allowed to roam the neighborhood alone at that age. I guess times were different then. So, I began knocking on the door frantically. The man quickly answered and even seemed happy to see us.

"Come on in," he said, smiling, his mustache much bigger than I remembered. We rushed inside and began all at once telling him why we were afraid. He made us feel comfortable. He gave us candy and soda and then started playing music. His house was neat but kind of grimy, the hardwood floors gleaming but at the same time looking like they had a thick layer of dust and could use a mopping.

"Come," the man said to each of us, tapping his hand on his seated legs, "sit on my lap."

We all took turns sitting on his lap. As I was there, he started to kiss me and put his tongue in my mouth. Yuck, it was gross. But I thought it was still better than having to face the angry maintenance man. I tried to laugh it off and move away from him, but I really didn't know what to do.

I was four. It's important that you not forget this.

I repeatedly tried to move away from the man, but he grabbed me, turned up his music really loud and led me into the back, to his bathroom. I guess I was his child of choice.

I don't know if I knew what was going to happen next. I don't remember being afraid at first, until he pulled my pants down. When he did, I immediately pulled them back up, but then he just pulled them back down. He then took a glob of what I believe was Vaseline and wiped it in between my butt cheeks. What happened next was horrifying and extremely painful. He pulled his pants down and sat on the side of the bathtub.

That's when it happened.

He pulled me down onto his erect penis and penetrated me anally. I screamed, but no one heard me. Now I know why he turned the music up so loud. I jumped up in horror, pulled my pants up and ran out of the bathroom to my unknowing friends.

"Let's go!" I said.

"Why?" Lajuan asked. "What's wrong?"

"Nothing. Let's go."

"But . . ."

"Let's go! I'm not playing!"

I just knew we had to get out of that apartment before the candy man found me and took me back into the bathroom, which would have been worse than anything the maintenance man could do to us. We left. As soon as we saw the coast was clear, I ran all the way home, terrified, my heart beating really fast, fear gripping me.

I was four.

As soon as I walked through the door of my house, my mother wanted us to leave.

"Let's go," she said.

We had planned to go to the mall, and she was going to buy me a ring. I was excited about that, but it was competing with a nasty, wet, sticky feeling in my underwear.

"I need to change," I said.

"Why?" she wanted to know.

I didn't feel like I could answer that question. If I did, I knew Mom would get mad at me. After all, it was my fault. Why did I take the janitor's mop? Why did I go into a strange man's apartment? If I hadn't taken the mop and angered the maintenance man, I wouldn't have had to hide. And then the candy man couldn't have done such an awful thing to me.

But Mom knew something was up. She wouldn't let it go. Mother's instinct, I guess. What she thought was that I had peed on myself.

"No," I assured her, "I didn't pee on myself." I ran to my room and quickly changed my underwear. As we got in the car and drove to the mall, the interrogation continued.

"Well, then, what is it? Why did you have to go change your underwear?"

"Nothing!" I insisted.

We got to the stoplight around the corner before I agreed to fess up. But I wanted to bargain first. "Okay," I said, "if I tell you, do you promise to still get me the ring?"

"No," she replied, "I make no promises. Tell me anyway—NOW!"

"Okay," I said. "We hid the maintenance man's mop, and he came chasing after us. So we went to hide in this other building and got inside this man's apartment, and then he gave us candy and soda and made me sit on his lap and kissed me with his tongue, and then he took me to the bathroom and pulled down my pants and wiped some stuff inside my butt and then pulled me down on his private, but then I jumped up and we ran out of his place. That's why I needed to change my underwear. Am I in trouble? Am I going to get a whupping? Are you still going to get me the ring?" I asked all of these things at once.

As soon as everything was out of my mouth, my mother screeched to a stop and made a u-turn in the middle of the street. Next thing I knew, we were back at the house and she had called my stepdad, who was a Secret Service agent. Within a few minutes, there were police all over the place in my home.

I'm sure that they asked me a lot of questions about what happened, but to be honest, I must have blocked it all out, as I have no memory of it. I do, however, remember that this team of guys with special clothes and guns went to the candy man's apartment. I had to go with them to point out his place. They surrounded it with their weapons out. It was like something out of a movie. I had to go down to the police station to identify him and give a statement.

It turned out that the candy man was from Mexico and in the country illegally. They deported him. That was the end of him forever. I never even knew his name. But the nightmare he gave me has never gone away.

I also never got the ring.

2 I AM NOT MY HAIR

MY MOTHER PUT A JHERI curl in my hair when I was in the second grade. You remember the Jheri curl? It was this permanent-wave hairstyle invented by the hairdresser Jheri Redding (hey, you think I can't do research?) and was popular with the black community in the Eighties and early Nineties. It makes your hair look kind of glossy and loose. And when I was seven, that's how my mother thought I should look.

Mind you, this was NOT a popular look for a second-grader. But I didn't have a lot of say in the matter.

Actually, the main reason my mother did it is because the chemical you use in the Jheri-curl process makes your hair more manageable. See, I didn't have that nice, fine white-girl textured hair like my sisters Krystal and Talia. I had a mixture of my mom's fine white-girl hair and my dad's extremely coarse (what people often call *nappy*) hair, so as a result, my mom didn't want to have to deal with it.

But you know, if you put a chemical like that in an *adult's* hair, you'd have to regularly care for it, go to the hairdresser and make sure it's treated, because otherwise it will break your hair off with split ends. So, in other words, my mother was asking a second-grader to take care of something she wasn't really prepared to do herself.

I mean, with a Jheri curl, you have to put this activator in it to keep it moisturized. You'd have to sleep with a plastic cap on. What little kid wants to go through all that fuss for her hair? Maybe in 2021, when looks mean everything, thanks to social media, but certainly not back in the Eighties. But Mama didn't want to be bothered doing it, either, so there's the problem.

Anyway, this went on for some years. My mama would complain about how my hair looked. It was so hurtful. I always felt like the ugly duckling in comparison to my mom and sisters, and most of this feeling came from how my mother criticized both my weight and my hair. The rest of how I felt came from the cruel kids at school.

Flash forward to sixth grade. Now I'm 12, but I guess I'm still not taking care of my far-too-mature hair the way she wanted me to. So, one night, just like a scene out of *Mommie Dearest*, she woke me up out of a dead sleep. She had a plan that I had not been filled in on.

"Wake up!" she yelled.

"What? What's going on?"

"We're gonna give you a haircut," she informed me.

"Huh?" I grunted, still half-asleep and not at all comprehending.

"I'm tired of you not taking care of your hair."

Now I was suddenly wide awake, as if someone had just taken a cattle prod to my brain.

"Wait, what? What do you mean?"

"I mean you don't know how to take care of your own hair, so I'm gonna take care of it for you! Right now!"

I couldn't believe what I was hearing. I was exhausted coming out of probably what was my REM sleep and horrified at the same time.

My mother was stoic and resolute: "Come on now." I was crying and I couldn't stop. I didn't understand what I could have done to justify her doing this to me in the middle of the night.

"But, but why?" I asked. The next thing I knew, we were in the downstairs bathroom. (There was only a shower in the second-floor bathroom.) She had me lean over the bathtub (something about trauma and bathrooms I guess) as she began washing my hair. I was crying hysterically, and then came the infamous phrase that my sisters and I laugh about now but that crushed me back then: "CRYING AIN'T GONNA DO NOTHING BUT GET YOU SLAPPED!"

So there I was, having to suck it up and allow this traumatic moment to happen. Once that part was over, we moved into the kitchen (the black family's salon). Mom blow-dried my hair, and then pulled out an electric razor and began shaving my head as if I were her little boy. For a minute, I thought, "This has to be a nightmare. I'm really still asleep." But once I convinced myself it was real, I started crying again. And crying. And crying.

"Don't you be cryin' and carryin' on," Mama threatened. "I told you before that cryin' is only gonna get you slapped!"

She didn't slap me. But she didn't stop, either. She cut my hair till maybe there was only an inch left, a total short, boy cut. I looked in the mirror when she was done and couldn't believe that what I was looking at was me. I didn't recognize myself.

I went back to bed, but I never fell back asleep. I was too busy dreading what was coming in school that morning. No big deal, right? Just a sixth-grader looking like a freak while everybody stared at me and judged. I'd rather have been dead. But dying wasn't an option at that moment.

Later that morning, I tried everything to help me look more like a little girl. I grabbed some fashion combs (which were really popular back then) and slicked my hair up on the sides. Fooling around with my hair made me late for school. OMG!!! Now there would be ALL EYES ON ME walking in that door. Everyone was already in their seats. And as soon as I entered, just like I feared, everyone's eyes shot to me like my hair was a magnet and their looks were steel.

I was humiliated, and it was all my mother's fault. Messing with a 12-year-old girl's hair is about the most traumatic thing that can happen to her.

Shit. I just wanted to disappear.

So, there I was, walking into Mr. Hall's class. He looked at me with a surprised expression. I decided I had to say something. The silence was killing me.

"Good morning, Mr. Hall," I said.

"Good morning, Angie," he said politely.

"Do you like my hair?" I asked.

"Do *you* like it?" Mr. Hall asked back.

"Yeah," I lied.

I mean, what else was I going to say? "No, I think I look like a boy, but my mother decided to do the most traumatic and abusive thing imaginable to me, something that will stay with me forever and force me to later write a memoir where I expose her big, blue uglies over this incident."

That wasn't going to come out of my mouth.

Fortunately, there was an open seat beside Leslie, and I took it. Leslie had very short hair, too, so it was a safety thing. She looked at me and smiled.

"You like your hair?"

"Yeah, I guess."

Leslie had a chemical in her hair and some type of condition that prevented it from growing. It was good to sit beside someone who was having an even worse hair day, or hair life, than me.

I got through it. But even sitting here writing this, I feel the pain and the hurt and the embarrassment all over again, like it was yesterday. I don't think my mother even conceived just how cruel her doing that was, particularly so impulsively in the middle of the night. This moment and many others experienced with Mama definitely left an indelible mark on my spirit and a lifelong battle with body image issues.

My mother never did THAT again. But she didn't have to. Once was more than enough.

3 MOMMIE DEAREST

IF IT ISN'T ALREADY OBVIOUS, my mama has never been the cuddly, touchy-feely type. She's probably the reason I was indirectly motivated to write this autobiography. Show me somebody who had a great relationship with their mother and was inspired to put together their life story. I'll wait.

My mother was, and still is, beautiful. Fair-skinned. Fine hair. She had what black people call "good hair." My sisters and I have often been mistaken for being her sisters instead of her daughters. You know what they say, "Black don't crack" LOL! (Now that I think about it, who is "they," anyway?)

While I was growing up, Joanna "Joan" Herndon (formerly Lawson, formerly Bowman, formerly Russell, formerly Johnson, now just plain formerly) was withholding and never much fun. I mean, I was no picnic, either. I was rebellious. I was pissed off a lot. But she was just not what you would call a nurturing mother.

She was the product of a mother who wasn't very nurturing herself. See how that works? Her mom catered to her boys, not the girls. My mother often tells the story of how she had to walk around with cardboard in the holes of her shoes to keep her feet dry, all because her mother opted to give money to her older brother for a brim instead of new shoes for her.

As a result, my mother was all about making sure my sisters and I had "things" and didn't grow up like she had.

This is all you need to know: my grandmother once left her baby son (my Uncle Reggie) on the doorstep of the home of my grandfather's niece (named Nanny). She put her infant boy down, knocked on the door, and walked away, understanding that she lacked the means to care for a second child at the time. I could probably write another book about the life of my grandmother. It's very dark and complicated, also not discussed. It's another one of those family secrets or mysteries that keeps us all in the prison of our own minds, especially the women in our family.

Anyway, Nanny discovered this baby, ran out to the street, saw my grandmother walking away, and called after her, "Wait a minute, come back!" She came back. They had a talk, and after hearing her story, Nanny assured her, "We can work this out." She invited my grandmother and her two kids (my Uncle Reggie and Aunt Geraldine) to live with them.

Upon my grandfather visiting his sister and niece one day, he met my grandmother and found out what was going on. They ended up dating, falling in love, and getting married. They were nineteen years apart. It's pretty heartwarming, except for, you know, the whole abandoning-her-child part.

My grandfather was one amazing man. I still think about him. He was very nurturing toward me. He called me his "little Monk Monk." I remember visiting him, crawling onto his lap and being the only one that could comb his very fine hair (atop his soft scalp). I felt loved and safe with him. I could always run into the warm security of his loving arms and away from my mom and dad if ever I was in trouble. I really miss him.

Back to Mom! My mama Joan was a provider with a capital "P." She worked for the Washington Metropolitan Area Transit Authority (or WMATA), which paid her union wages, great benefits, and ultimately a generous retirement. She left at a high rate of pay and with no bills. She still draws a six-figure income and Social Security, with no bills to speak of. A pretty sweet deal.

My mother was also a compulsive gambler and very good at it. We had great Christmases as a result. She would invite people over and have these marathon card-playing parties that would last for days on end. These women wouldn't sleep, just sit at the table and play cards all night. Poker. Blackjack. Spades. Bid Whist. I don't even know what they were playing half the time.

All I remember is, there was big money involved. None of that penny-ante stuff. The grownups participating would pay my older sister and I money to run and get them food from the store, because they didn't want to have to leave that table. I recall going to bed with my mom playing cards and waking up to her STILL at that table playing cards.

To this day, I'm not really sure how much money Mama earned from her gambling. But I'll bet she made more than she lost. She not only played cards at home, she frequented Dover Downs Casino quite often as well.

My stepdad, Tim, helped bring some joy to my childhood. But he brought along pain, too. When I got into trouble, he would punish me by whipping me with a razor strap all over my naked body. But if it weren't for Tim, my big sister Krystal, my little sister Talia, and I (in the middle) wouldn't have gone to the movies and McDonald's all the time. We wouldn't have gone on trips. Tim was a Secret Service agent, so we traveled quite a bit.

Mama was too busy working and gambling to be as big a part of our life as Tim was. She didn't go to movies with us or attend school plays or talent shows often, if at all. I remember being envious of the little girls at school whose parents were so involved with the PTA and all their activities. I still look with envy at women today who have great relationships with their moms. It's something I never had, and I'm pretty sure I never will.

It turned out that Tim didn't come into my life until I was two, when my mother remarried after splitting with my biological father,

formerly known as Randolph Bowman (now Bowman-Horton), *a.k.a.* Reds. But that's a story for later.

This gets a little complicated. My sister Krystal actually had a different father. But Mama split from him because he was a drug dealer and he personally indulged as well. And to her credit, my mother didn't want that influence around us. Soon after, she met Reds. Reds adopted Krystal, and she took his last name. This is where the heartwarming part would happen, except that Reds would become a drug dealer for a time, too.

My mother instilled in us a zero tolerance for drugs. It's one of the positive things she gave us, along with the bond that she helped to build between my sisters and me. As I write these words, I have not indulged in drug use aside from a few edibles. I owe her for that. Another wonderful quality of hers was that she insisted no kid ever be treated poorly due to mistakes made by the adults around them.

That's kind of it for the positive stuff. I know that may sound like an awful thing to say, but if you could see the hole in my soul and in my heart as a result of her rejection of me, then you would extend me some grace.

In general, Joan was/is controlling and negative. We had a volatile relationship from the word GO. She's a very toxic individual. Part of her anger could stem from abuse that she suffered at the hands of an older brother, my creepy Uncle Reggie. He was the uncle that everybody stayed away from. Every family has one. He was the one who was always super inappropriate, who tried to kiss you on your mouth. YUCK! You never let your kids sit on his lap.

I found out about the abuse my mom suffered from a discussion with my Uncle Kirk, whom I love dearly. There's always one family member who is privy to all the stories, who knows where all the bodies are buried. In my family, that's Kirk. He also told me that he thought my biological dad, Reds, was the only man my mother ever truly loved, and that she probably took things out on me because of that.

My anger peaked after I discovered that Krystal and I had different fathers. As I got older and we began to clash more and more, I tried to get away from my mother as much as I could. I lived with Reds for a short period of time. I stayed with my grandfather. I stayed with my grandmother. I stayed with my best friend.

Other people have told me, and I tend to agree, that my mom was and remains jealous of me. I was a very free-spirited girl, and I'm a free-spirited woman today. I didn't allow her to control me, nor do I allow it today, and I'm

sure that drove her crazy. I think she resented that I wouldn't let her change me, that I didn't listen to her demand that I get a job at Metro for the pension.

But, oh man, she tried like crazy to get under my skin whenever she could, and it worked. Thankfully, I would still come out on top, no matter how many times she was determined to break me. But it wasn't easy. It's come with a lot of tears and a lot of abuse that I would allow from others. It was just simply my love language. It was what I was used to. It was what I thought I deserved.

At every turn, my mother seemed to take pleasure in sabotaging me. I'll give you an example. She asked my eldest daughter, Kelsey, a couple of years back, "So, Kelsey, are you dating?"

"No," Kelsey replied, "Mom wants me to focus on my school and making sure I'm really secure in my future and things like that."

"Well," my mother said, "I don't know why she wouldn't let you have a boyfriend. She was always dating guys and running wild in the street and stuff like that. She shouldn't tell you that you can't date."

Of course, this got back to me. How in the hell is this helpful in any way? She tries to take the focus off something positive and make it look like I don't want my child to have any fun.

Why would I want to engage with a woman like that?

It has sometimes been so bad that Talia's therapist once told her she needed to disconnect from our mother, and she listened and stopped contact, off and on. I have taken this advice myself, and let me tell you, it has brought me so much peace.

Talia and I have asked our mother to go to counseling with us, but she refused, telling us we were crazy. Every time we let her back in, we deceived ourselves into thinking it was going to be better, but it never was. That's just the way it happens when you're dealing with a covert narcissist.

There is an established pattern of complete, control-freaky game playing with my mother. The fact that Mama is financially set is something she has used to feed her games. She'll offer to do things for you but demand to call the shots for how it gets done. If she's going to foot the bill for getting your house painted, it needs to be painted her way. If it isn't, she'll renege on paying. It never fails.

She offered to get Kelsey a nice Apple laptop three years ago. A few days later, she changed her mind. What happened?

"Well, I just don't think that you need it," she told Kelsey. "So I'm not going to put my money in for it."

I don't know if she felt taken advantage of or what. But if she did, she shouldn't have offered to pay for it in the first place. Same thing happened when there was a situation where my daughter lost a portion of her funding for school. We ended up having to pay for her college dorm. Kelsey was trying to work it out on her own, without telling us, but she got herself into a situation and fell behind three months on the rent. She was going to be evicted.

Kelsey called my mother, and my mother was like, "Don't you worry, Kelsey, you are going to be the first one in our family to graduate college. I don't want you to have to worry about anything. I'm going to take care of this. I'm going to put up my money and pay for your dorm."

When my mom called to inform me of this, I was like, "Well, Mom, I don't want you to have to do that on your own. She's my daughter. I want to contribute. If you're offering help, that's great, but I also want to put in something. So, I did. Then she said, "Going forward, let's split this half and half."

Of course, a month into the agreement, she backed out, as expected: "I'm no longer doing this. You'll have to take care of this by yourself."

If you're a grandchild who wants to get a car, unless you get the kind of car she wants you to get, forget about it. She promises the money. Two weeks later, she unpromises. Bang! This happened more times than I can count.

Joan used money as a weapon to assert power and control. Everyone in the family was her victim at one time or another. My sisters. Her brother. Everyone. It got to the point where no one would take her help because there were too many strings attached—and you knew she would change her mind, anyhow.

I've always gone the opposite way of my mother, who supplied a very effective reverse role model for me in raising and nurturing my own children. I chose that other route. I was determined to always be there for my kids, in a way my mother rarely was for me. I'm the mom who has been involved in their school, played games with them, taken them on trips, and wanted to spend time with them.

I used my relationship with my mother as motivation to make myself a better mother, so in that sense it was a blessing in disguise. I made it a point to be open and honest with my kids about all my big, ugly mistakes. My mom was never like that. She always made it a point to try to look like she had been the perfect child growing up and was now the perfect mother. She's never owned anything about herself that could be viewed as negative.

I've also lived my adulthood much differently from her in that I never wanted to be tied to a desk and a nine-to-five job. Not me. The longest I held a job was six years, and that was at the Recording Industry Association of America. I would hardly call that work, the way my brother Hakim and I ran that place. I may not have managed my money the way that my mother wanted me to, but I spent it on the kids. I put them in dance. I put them in baseball. I paid for the nice vacations. That's something Mama didn't always agree with.

She kind of made her own bed in terms of her kids and grandchildren. She's not that warm and fuzzy grandmother that wants the grandkids for the summer. The one time my kids did spend a few days with her, they ALL were miserable. She did nothing but complain and wouldn't allow them to just be kids. That was the last time they were alone with her.

Mom still has a solid relationship with my sister Krystal, who has consistently cast herself as the protector in our family. She's always said, "That's still our mother." She tried to empathize with her and protect her no matter what, and I understand and respect her for it. She's prided herself on being the glue that holds things together. That's never going to be me. I'm never good enough for my mother.

I've had to monitor and oversee my children's relationship with their grandmother. I had no choice. At every opportunity, she tried to turn my children against me and say awful things about me. I've had to do everything in my power to shut that off. She's still allowed to see the grandkids, but I'll never be comfortable with her seeing them alone—even after they're grown.

You know how siblings argue over which child is their parents' favorite in a family? Krystal and Talia and I don't do that. We already know Krystal's the favorite. Instead, we argue over which daughter is the *least* favorite. And it became clear in 2020 that it was me.

A conversation with Talia in the middle of the COVID pandemic last year confirmed it.

"You must have broken Mama's heart somehow," Talia told me after having just gotten off the phone with our mother.

"Why?" I asked.

"Because she lets you have so much power over her that you're all she thinks about," she replied. "The only thing she does is complain about and trash you over stuff. She must really, really have a thing for you."

Talia's point was that I was such an obsession for Mama that I had to be her favorite. I saw it the opposite way.

"What it's about," I reasoned to my sister, "is that I'm the only one she's never been able to control at any point in my life. And for someone like her, that's completely crazy-making. It frustrates the shit out of her."

The flip side of that is complete jealousy. My mother has wished she could be free and easy like me, but her negative way of looking at the world has never allowed it.

There was this one time when, on the advice of Talia, I read a letter out loud to my mother, crying, regarding my feelings about her. But she so lacks compassion that she can't hear you even when your heart is bleeding. I was in tears, but it elicited not a single bit of emotion from her. It was positively sociopathic. No "Angie, I'm really sorry you feel that way. I never meant to make you feel like that." Instead, it was, "You're crazy, Angie. And you're dramatic." It was just horrible.

Talia tried the same thing, also in tears, and the very same thing happened. She was just like, "Mom, you're not hearing me. I'm trying to tell you about me and how I feel in our relationship, and you keep going back to Angie and all that you've done for her and what she doesn't do and how she never calls and blah blah blah."

It's like she carries around this big ball of anger and resentment over the fact she had these kids and it put a damper on her life.

Krystal has always acted like more of a mother to me than Joan has. And then, because she's envious that I'm the mother she could never be, that I've raised my kids in the total opposite manner of how Mama did, she worked to discredit me at every turn.

All of this said, I finally have peace with it all. The fact that I've not spoken to my mother much lately is fine by me. It's the way things need to be in order to protect my heart and to just keep my sanity. I believe it may be this way for the rest of my life. When you're met with so much judgment and bitterness, at some point you just have to surrender and leave it all behind.

You've heard about the definition of insanity, right? It's repeating the same actions over and over and expecting different results. Well, I no longer expect anything to change when it comes to Mommie Dearest. Maybe that means I'm sane after all.

4 SCHOOL DAZE

I DID WELL IN SCHOOL. I was a good student. I made the honor roll. But for some reason, I was placed in the lowest reading group at Bladensburg Elementary School in Bladensburg, Maryland.

One day, I approached my teacher, Mrs. Brazil, and told her, "I don't like this book. Why am I having to read out of it?"

"What do you mean, you don't like this book?" she asked.

"Well, the words are too easy," I told her.

"Do you think that you can read *this*?" she asked, handing me another book.

I started reading it fluently, right in front of her. That earned me a spot in the highest reading group. Had I not spoken up for myself, I probably would have gone my entire grade school career on the lowest reading level and never been tested or challenged. Lesson learned.

Mrs. Brazil was shocked at my reading ability. After that, I qualified for all the spelling bees and started winning them. So, as far as academics, things were fine.

But I wasn't popular. No way. I was the girl with the Jheri curl. I was overweight. I knew the popular people and how to interact with them, but I wasn't cool. I wasn't the pretty one. My best friend in grade school was a white girl named Teria Wilson, and she accepted me for who I was. She also didn't mind getting a little crazy together.

I remember this one day, while I was in the sixth grade, when we didn't go to school. There were four of us who skipped: Teria, me, this guy Keith, and another friend named Marcy,

We went to Teria's house, and of course her parents weren't home.

At some point, Teria said, "Let's have sex."

Remember, we're all 11 or 12. Not the kind of thing you'd expect a girl that age to suggest.

So, first Teria and Keith, and then Marcy and Keith did the deed, while I watched.

What's most wrong with this picture? Oh, yeah. It's the fact I didn't participate. It was never my turn. I was evidently there to play the voyeur.

It wasn't because I didn't want to join in, although I really had no interest in Keith. He was the dirty boy who picked and ate his boogers. It was mainly that there was no interest in me being part of it because I was The Black Girl. Joining in was never presented as an option. That's the only explanation I've ever been able to come up with.

My friends were all under the covers, but they were doing it right there in front of me. I represented the racial divide.

That divide continued when I went to William Wirt Middle School in Riverdale, Maryland, in the seventh grade. The black kids all hung with the black kids. The white kids all hung with the white kids. These were unwritten rules, but they were set in stone.

Meanwhile, because of the divide, me and Teria stopped being best friends. Just

. . . stopped. Poof. Done, like overnight. It wasn't anything we ever discussed. It just happened, and you rolled with it and never questioned it.

We had to be bused to William Wirt, because they closed down our neighborhood middle school. As a middle-class kid from the suburbs, I got my first taste of what impoverishment looked like. It was a different world. Though the school itself was mixed, with all kinds of kids from all situations tossed together, it opened my eyes wide.

Suddenly, I had issues with gangs. You had all these girls from this particular hood. There was the M Team, the Baby M Team, the Lady M Team. The one thing they all had in common was they were fighters. I wasn't.

Now I was surrounded by all these tough chicks, and this one girl starts picking on me. I was scared to death. So, I remember bringing a big metal disc with me as a weapon, for protection. I put it in my purse to have it handy because I knew this girl wanted to fight me, and I needed to defend myself.

I thought about the movie *Bad Boys* with Sean Penn. You know the part where he was in jail and filled a pillowcase with soda cans to use as a weapon? Yeah, that was gonna be me with the metal disc in my purse. LOL! I was prepared to swing away.

Who R U?

Sure enough, I arrived at school and this girl was waiting to get me. That's when I met a girl named Sabrina, who would become my best friend. She had my back all through school after that.

"You don't want to fight Angie," she told the other girl, whose name was Poochie. Poochie! I was scared of a girl named Poochie! They both were a part of the same gang, so Sabrina was able to provide protection for me. Basically, I was now accepted because Sabrina said so. I was instantly untouchable.

That intervention resulted in the girl making peace with me. The fight didn't go down. And Brie (as I would come to call her) said to me, "As long as you're with me, you're gonna be alright." We're still best friends to this day. She is my Ride or Die. The toughness that I've learned, I've gotten from her.

They used to call her "Sabruno" because she was the only girl any of us knew who fought like a dude. Most girls had catfights and did that windmill swinging thing, but Brie fought straight-up. She was a boxer, so you didn't want to mess with her. She knew how to take you out. She was no-nonsense.

There were a couple of other run-ins where someone would come after me, or Brie had an issue with somebody. I had her back, too. I got into quite a few fights myself, though it wasn't me starting them. A lot of it stemmed from reverse racism, because I'm the light-skinned black girl. All the girls wanted to fight me due to that jealousy—the skin, and of course my glowing personality.

I went to William Wirt, then to Bowie High School in Bowie, Maryland, starting in ninth grade. I began performing at Bowie in the drama club. Sang in the talent show, too. Actually, I went to multiple high schools, because I was leaving Mom, going to Dad, then to Granddad. High school was a whole back-and-forth thing.

But you know, my most indelible school memory is probably something that didn't have anything to do with school itself really. I remember it like it was yesterday. It was 1986, and I was in the eighth grade. It was when the Space Shuttle Challenger exploded, and all of us at Wirt watched it live together.

We were all so excited because Christa McAuliffe, a teacher, was going up to be a part of the crew. This was a big deal because we all saw the selection process for her and how they settled on Christa. There was a big campaign for who would be chosen, all of the exercises they had to endure, the conditioning of their bodies, all of that.

We were all standing and glued to the live broadcast of the launch. It was like this huge event. I was in Mrs. Howard's Spanish class, but a bunch of our classrooms merged together to watch it.

And then there was this giant explosion, and everything got real quiet.

"What was *that*?" someone asked.

"I don't know," someone else answered.

"*Obviously, a major malfunction,*" calmly said the man on the TV.

We were all just sitting there staring at the screen, shocked and confused. A few of the more immature kids laughed and joked: "Hey, it blew up, man!"

Some of us started to cry. It was unbelievable. How could Christa die? She was a teacher. Teachers don't die in rocket ships. As it all started to sink in, we grew more and more devastated. We saw the shuttle break off into pieces and head toward the water, and we knew it was all over.

What we didn't know until later on was that the astronauts didn't die in that initial explosion. They stayed alive until the main cabin where the people were housed hit the water 2 minutes and 45 seconds later. We all thought at the time that they must have died instantly. They didn't. They knew what was coming for almost three full minutes.

I remember listening to the manuscript of what was said in the moments right before their demise, as read by Donnie Simpson, a legendary radio personality. It was chilling to hear. Once all of them started to feel the heat enter into the shuttle, they knew they were doomed. They started to beg and plead for their lives. A female voice said, "No, please God, not like this," and then a male voice started to recite The Lord's Prayer. I can't imagine the fear that must have gripped them all.

That I can remember this so vividly 35 years later says all you need to know about what a trauma it was to watch. I still get a chill just thinking about it.

5 WHAT'S MY NAME?

MY NAME IS SPELLED "ANGELIA," but it's pronounced, "An-juh-lie." (It happens to mean "Messenger of God," and I'm good with that.) I think my mom didn't really know how to spell at the time, or maybe she was under the influence of something. I don't know. I know she was really sick while in the hospital giving birth to me. There is still some discrepancy about the pronunciation of my name. All I can tell you is that no one who sees my name for the first time ever knows how to correctly pronounce it. I'm not even sure how to do it myself.

I'll tell you what else is really funny. I spelled my name incorrectly all the way through the sixth grade—without the "i" near the end.

I only found this out accidentally, when I continued to receive mail from Scholastic Books with my name being spelled Angelia—and decided I'd finally confront Mama about it.

"Mom," I said, "why do they keep sending me these books but spell my name wrong? That's not how you spell it."

"Yes, it is," she said, looking at the label.

"Huh? What are you talking about? No, it isn't."

"Yes, it surely is," she insisted. "I'm your mother and I named you. I think I would know how to spell your name."

"But," I shot back, "I've been spelling it A-N-G-E-L-A my whole life." (Of course, my whole life to this point was only 11 years—but still.)

"Well, you've been wrong, young lady."

What? What? Who has an argument with their mother over the correct spelling of their name? Why didn't *she* ever notice I was spelling it wrong? Probably because I was getting A's and B's, and she never needed to look at my papers or report cards.

But talk about an identity crisis. Who the hell *was* I, anyway? I guess I was Angie. The rest didn't matter. As I went into the music industry, I was known as "Angelia" because it was much less common then Angie AND a great conversation starter.

That wasn't the only identity crisis I suffered. Growing up, my last name was Bowman, and so was my sister Krystal's. I didn't know that we had different dads until one fateful day when Arnelda, Krystal's newfound sister, blurted it out.

But how did we have the same last name? It was all so confusing back then, but I definitely recall always feeling like the outcast, the black sheep, the ugly duckling. Tim was Talia's dad, and since she was biologically his and she was the youngest, she was a spoiled brat!

I know that many parents claim you can love children the same, even if they aren't yours biologically. I beg to dIffer. No matter how much you try to treat them all equally, I believe there are connections and bonds between a biological parent with a child that allow them to have more patience and compassion toward them than those who are adopted or a step relation. At least, that's the way I always imagined it was supposed to be. But as I've made clear, I don't feel like my mother and I have ever bonded and don't think we ever will.

6 IDENTITY CRISIS

But let me just confuse you a little bit more. Maybe a *lot* more.

The girls I considered my sisters when I was growing up were Krystal and Talia. I was in the middle. We all came out of the same mother. But we also all had different biological dads.

I'm the daughter of Randolph "Reds" Bowman Horton. He adopted my older sister Krystal. Talia's father is Tim. It turns out that Reds also has kids named Monica, Monique, Roderick, and Randy, my half-siblings. Then there is Katisha, who was a product of my dad's affair, before he and my mother split. Krystal's birth father is actually Arnold, who is also the father of Arnelda, Krystal's long-lost sister, who infiltrated our home when I was young, posing as a cousin—until we found out that she was in fact Krystal's sister.

Take notes. There will be a quiz on all this later. (JUST KIDDING, LOL)

There is some great drama involved in it, as you might imagine. Katisha—who is now a professional dancer and choreographer—came out of Reds' affair. He was cheating on my mother both before she was pregnant with me and while she was carrying me. My dad had countless affairs (or what we would call today a "SLIDE, JUMP OFF, SIDE CHICK"), all a product of how popular he was due to his basketball career.

I remember my mom once telling me the story of when she found Katisha's mom hiding naked in the closet of their house. Then there was the time that my mom chased my dad down in the rain while pregnant with me, after finding another woman in the car with him. That apparently led to a big fight out in the rain. See, my mom was also a fighter! She may not have looked it, but she was one tough cookie. She still is. She may give us the blues, but she would never let anyone else mess with us. She will lay down her life. Still.

Anyway, I'm the second-eldest of Mom's children and the eldest of Dad's. Krystal and Talia are the ones I'm close to. As I mentioned earlier, Krystal has always been there as the family defender, the voice of reason when things go screwy. She really has been more of a mother to me then my own mother has.

I've periodically tried to build a relationship with my half-sisters, Monica and Monique, but it's hard. The two are fraternal twins. Monica has always been pretty uppity, selfish, and disloyal, in my opinion. I don't mesh well with people like that.

Monique has been the fun, cool twin, and she tries to connect with me and my kids from time to time, but it remains short-lived. Everything always has to be about them. If it wasn't, they weren't interested.

The sisters worked at R.N. Horton's (the R.N. stood for Rufus Nathaniel) Funeral Home for years (if you want to call it "work") and abused their positions of "daughter" to the boss for many years, nearly bringing financial ruin to the legacy that my father would eventually carry out on their behalf.

The girls would leave in the middle of the workday to get their hair done. They would skip work for local excursions and lavish trips around the world on my father's dime—or should I say, the funeral home's dime. They were great at running up their personal tab and the business into the ground, until my father hired a woman to help whip everything and everyone (including them) into shape. They no longer work there. That's why it's still in business.

None of the original Horton family members (besides the lovely Ella, the cousin of the founder) could have done what my dad ended up doing for founder R.N. Horton's legacy. If it were not for him, Horton's Funeral Home would have folded decades ago.

As for my brothers Randy and Roderick, I have always held them near and dear to my heart. I have fond memories of my little brother Roderick, and as an adult he has always shown me love and respect. He has been on a career path to become a gangsta rapper for several years now. I'm not sure if that will ever pan out. It would have been nice to see him work alongside my dad and run the family business, but I don't think that's going to happen. As for Randy, the poor guy has led a troubled life, in and out of jail, on and off the streets, only to get strung out on heroin. He once told me that this drug is the devil and that NO ONE beats it successfully.

I know that isn't true for everyone, but in Randy's case, it is. It breaks my heart to see him like that. He was once a very handsome young man, but now he looks so old, used up, and downtrodden, like a walking zombie. I love him and wish his life were different.

Last but not least, there's Katisha. She and I have had a nice relationship over the years. Distance has kept us from being closer, I'm sure. We have a lot in common, but the main thing we share is the feeling of abandonment from our dad. See, we didn't have him growing up while the others did, but I believe it's made us stronger.

The two of us are still working on our relationship with our dad and have come a long way. Family can be a tough thing. I've always felt like I got lucky with Krystal and Talia, though, that's for sure. We share a bond like no other. I would go to the ends of the earth for them. The other sibs? Not so much. It is what it is.

7 THE STEP-IN DAD

My mother split from my biological father when I was still a baby, so I grew up with Tim playing the role of my daddy. I honestly don't have memories of my bio father before the eighth grade, although a heated conversation with my sister Krystal while writing this book gives me reason to believe that maybe I should have.

I had no reason to think any differently about who my father was at a young age because Tim was all I really knew. He got with my mom when I was a toddler. He was a decent-looking man, darker-skinned, big eyes, small head, very tall and (in terms of his parenting style) STRICT! Like my daddy Reds, he was also a basketball player in high school and college.

I wasn't a well-behaved kid by any means. I was mischievous, rebellious, effervescent, gregarious, the little girl who wanted to be loved and just FIT IN. My personality always caused me to stand out. It still does. But I never felt pretty, loved, or popular, so I was constantly looking for ways to get attention. That strong desire always caused me to get into trouble, and my stepdad believed in corporal punishment. Therefore, I got a lot of spankings. And when I say spankings, I mean beatings.

Tim used to whip me with a razor strap, like the kind they have in barbershops. He would first tell me to get fully undressed and then he would beat me with it repeatedly while I was naked, all over my body. *Thwap! Thwap! Thwap! Thwap!* Oh my God, did that hurt. It was torturous. It would leave welts. This happened when I was 9, 10, 11 years old. It made me grow to hate him.

Thwap! Thwap! Thwap! Sting.

To my mother's credit, once she found out about the whuppings, she put a stop to the naked part. But she would still be okay with him doing this as long as my clothes weren't off. Today, we would call this child abuse. Back then, I guess it was known as discipline. Physical punishment. Something you did to keep your child in line. And that wasn't my only issue with my stepfather. Once it was clear that he wasn't my actual father, I wanted to go live with my real daddy.

When I was little, I thought it was my imagination that Tim favored Talia. But once I understood that she was his natural daughter and I wasn't, it all started to make sense.

Like I said earlier, when it's your kid instead of your stepkid, you tend to be more patient, more forgiving, more generous. It's just instinctive. And you have to make a conscious effort when it's someone who isn't your flesh and blood to be that same way.

Even so, we had plenty of good times with my stepdad. It was the simple things that left me with some fond memories of my childhood with him. We would go to the drive-in where he introduced me to kung fu and burritos. There were also countless rides to the dump in the back of his orange pickup truck. Man, that was fun! Too dangerous to do today, though. Different time.

We went on a lot of trips together, like to Ohio, Nashville, and Disney World. Tim was a Freemason, part of Prince Hall, so he toured around a lot with them, and we got to travel due to his career as a Secret Service agent. We traveled with the POTUS!

That's right. We traveled together with the President of the United States. I remember when Jimmy Carter was in office, and I was really young, like six or seven years old. We went to the White House a lot. I remember playing there with his daughter, Amy, and her dog. It was great.

But things got weird at the end of my mother's and Tim's relationship. From what I understood, Tim finally got fed up with all of Mom's gambling. I would later come to learn that it was also partially due to his infidelity while traveling with those Masons that made her not want to come home.

I mean, I just don't get it. My mom clearly is not perfect by any means, but damn, she was fine! How do you bring yourself to cheat on *that*? It's a vicious cycle that I later would have to endure as well. I feel as though Tim was lucky to even have gotten her in the first place.

But because Tim was the more present and available parent, he was able to convince us to actually leave my mom and go to live with him. One day, he completely cleaned out the house, rented a home, packed us up, left my mother a check on the stairs, and we drove off with him—no warning, no nothing. I was 14.

It's hard for me to imagine how traumatic that had to be for my mother to come home and have the whole house and her children gone. That deeply wounded her. Once we saw just how hurt she was, we hurt, too. But there was really no going back after that, although Tim tried. My mother was DONE!

Why did they finally split? Well, there was the cheating and the gambling, for starters. They obviously grew apart. Maybe she just completely shut down and shut him out. What-ever it was, Tim had the balls to leave and take us with him. When I think back on it, it's pretty insane.

8 ESTHER #1

To say that my mother wasn't helpful when it came to my relationships with the opposite sex would be a significant understatement. I wasn't The Pretty Girl back in my teens, and Mom did everything she could to tear me down and make me feel ugly.

After we moved with my stepdad Tim and left my mother, he had another girlfriend who moved in with us pretty quickly. This woman's being there for me would represent a turning point in my life. I really owe her a lot.

Her name was Esther Southern. I'll never forget what she did for me.

Some of the stuff sounds small now in context, but at the time it was huge. For instance, we had a conversation where she spoke to me about my hygiene issues. As a teenager, my clean-up skills weren't the best. I didn't have a mom who really taught me about those things.

There was a short period in my life where I had an issue with an odor, a discharge in my female region. I was showering, I was cleaning my private areas, but the smell still wouldn't go away. I was also heavier, and my thighs would rub together so badly that I would wear holes in the inner part of my jeans. This had gone on for some time. When I shared this with Esther, she told me that she had an incurable yeast infection or some other kind of condition where she would always have to use a tampon to help absorb the discharge and cause her to have an odor, too.

"You should see a doctor, Angie," she told me.

Esther took me to that first doctor's appointment, and I did indeed have an infection that they gave me an antibiotic to get rid of. It cured me. Without Esther, I have no idea how long the problem would have gone on. And on. Maybe forever.

She was a very sharp woman. Worked as a paralegal. She had a son and a daughter. They both came to live with us in our new home.

Esther told me I was beautiful. You have no idea how much that meant, because my mom and my sisters, they were the pretty ones with the nice hair.

"Don't ever let anybody tell you that you aren't beautiful," Esther told me. "You are incredibly beautiful. All you need to do is take care of yourself as a woman."

I listened to Esther. She took me to the hairdresser and taught me how to care for my hair. She brought me out shopping and taught me how to shop. She took me under her wing and gave me instruction on how to be a young woman, how to make the most of what I had. It gave me the confidence I completely lacked before.

"Man," my stepfather joked to her, "you should never have told Angie she was beautiful because now she thinks she's a goddamned prima donna!" Or maybe he wasn't joking. I will always remember that moment. I went from an ugly duckling to a beautiful swan.

In ninth grade, I began developing a sense of confidence and self-esteem that stays with me to this day, even more so now as a top Pure Romance consultant and leader of a multimillion-dollar team. By the time I got to twelfth grade, I had transformed. I was slim, trim, and sexy. This isn't to say I wasn't always looking for love in all the wrong places and searching for validation. I still wasn't the popular girl, the "IT" girl, or even part of the cool clique. But I carried myself differently. I knew I was *something*.

I have Esther Southern to thank for so much of what I became and have become. She ultimately split with my stepdad, and there were some things that transpired that left the family not completely loving her. From what I understand, Esther started to abuse Talia physically. She also had some run-ins with my mom, like the time my mom tried to hit Esther by driving the car up onto the lawn and into the house.

My family never really understood how I could hold Esther in such high regard and still be okay with her after some of the things they accused her of doing. I told them I had a different relationship with her and owe her a debt of gratitude, because she helped me to know my self-worth.

Do I doubt that what my family members say about Esther was true? No. If they say it happened, I have to believe them. All I know is that what she did for me was *life-changing*, and people change as well. Maybe something happened between she and Tim that caused her to mistreat Talia. I hate the thought of that, but I can't ever toss what she did for me to the side.

Thank you for everything, Esther.

9 ABUSE

I WAS VIOLATED FOR THE first time when I was four, as I wrote in Chapter 1, before I even knew what abuse meant. But it wasn't the last time. Not by a longshot. There was an uncle and two cousins who touched me inappropriately. And there were three different people in my family who molested me in total. That only includes the ones I can remember.

There was my Uncle Craig, my father's brother. I never told my dad about it at the time. Then there was my cousin Chester, my aunt's son, though we called him Uncle Chester for some reason.

I remember it like it was yesterday. I was eight. I recall that it was Christmastime. We were at my grandmother's apartment, a place where she lived for several years. My granddad, the one who called me Monk Monk, had

sadly passed away while my mother was still pregnant with Talia. We were all devastated by his loss. I will never forget walking into his bedroom and finding him the way we did.

With all of the family fun and the food this one day, I got sleepy and went to take a little nap. I walked in and laid on the bed, and I think my cousin Shaunie came with me to lay down, too.

There we were, and here came Chester. He climbed into bed, pulled down his pants, rubbed his penis on me, and started to fondle me.

Someone walked into the room and Chester jumped up. They were like, "What are you doing? Get away from her!"

"I wasn't doing anything," he said.

That was the only time this happened with Chester that I remember. But it creeped me out. When you have male family members who force themselves on you like that and keep doing it even when you say "No," it makes you feel so much less safe. You carry around this uneasy feeling that something isn't quite right.

Then there was another time when I was living with my Poppy. This was dad's dad. I was playing in the neighborhood with some friends, and there was this one guy named Lorenzo. We all thought he was so fine. He looked like Prince. He was also a nice guy, and a musician too.

I remember going to visit Lorenzo, but he wasn't home. His brother told me, "He'll be back in a little bit, so you can come in and wait." The brother took me upstairs into his room and showed me Lorenzo's music collection. And then, he forced himself on me. Like full-on rape.

This had happened to me so many times that it wasn't as if I even felt powerless anymore. It was worse than that. It felt *normal*, like something that was supposed to happen to me. When it occurs multiple times, it just becomes routine.

Did I report it? No, I didn't. Who would I tell? What would I say? I probably should never have been in the house with this guy in the first place. It felt embarrassing. I mean, knowing what I know now, of course, I wouldn't accept being raped as my fate, as my own fault. But back then, it just seemed like I had asked for it by putting myself in the situation.

Instead of reporting it, I just never went back around there ever again.

From the time I was still in my mid-teens, I loved hard, or at least thought I did. When I liked someone, I really wanted them to like me back, and guys preyed on and took advantage of that to get me into compromising positions.

There was this one guy who was wealthy and drove a fast car—I think it was a Dodge Viper. I had never been in a car that fast, and I was horrified by how recklessly he drove it, but I never said a word. We had gone to an event together, and he took me back to his house, which was this beautiful mansion. I was still a teenager. He was in his 30's. He wanted to have sex with me, and I told him, "No, I don't really know you like that yet." But he kept pushing it and pushing it, and of course one thing led to another.

"I just want to touch you . . ."

"I just want to kiss you . . ."

"I just want to put my hand there . . ."

"Oh, let me just play with it, touch it, kiss it . . ."

"Let me just . . . I'm not going to put it in . . ."

It kept going and going like this. The guy was smooth.

I remember lying there and feeling silently powerless, tears rolling down my cheeks. Fortunately, in this case, he saw my reaction and stopped. Somehow, his humanity kicked in. He got dressed. I got dressed. He took me home. And I never saw him again.

On some level, it connected with him that he was being an abusive asshole. It was the rare instance when how I responded was ultimately given credence and respected—too late, but still. It helped me to build a wall around me, a protective mechanism that inspired me to become the aggressor in bed. It's much more comfortable for me than allowing a partner to take control, even if it's well-intentioned.

The sexual molestations and assaults I endured drove me to become very promiscuous. It was a vibe that I emitted.

For example, when I was going to perform at the famed Apollo Theater in New York City, there was a guy working there, Antwan, who gave us a tour of the place—and I wound up hooking up with him. We quickly fell into a relationship from it. It was like something out of a movie.

I mean, picture this. I'm 19. Not long out of high school. This guy's showing me around the Apollo. I'm looking for a place to change clothes in the dressing room. I asked him to button up my dress. I turned around. Our eyes locked. We started to kiss, finally ripped our clothes off, and we did it *right there*. We hadn't known each other more than a few minutes. We had sex completely out of nowhere.

It turned out that Antwan wasn't a bad guy. We legitimately liked each other. But this was utterly impulsive and insane to have it go from 0 to 100 instantly. I traveled back and forth to New York to see him, but he had a baby on the way with a girlfriend he'd broken up with, and I didn't want to be bothered with that. Once the baby was born, I broke it off.

But right after that, I started getting hooked up with drug dealers—despite never doing any of the drugs (because it's too easy to lose control). Hooking up with drug dealers, though, was a different story. It was the hottest thing. If you didn't have one you were hooking up with, you were lame! I've always unfortunately had a thing for the bad boys. I wonder what that stemmed from? Hmm . . .

Once I started having kids of my own, as a mom, as a survivor of abuse, my thing became putting a safety mechanism into place for me and my children. But there's nothing foolproof that will protect your kids, particularly when it happens under your own roof.

Kelsey was violated in our home at the tender age of seven.

It was a horrible thing to have occurred. Here I thought I had educated my sons on what I had been through and why it was important for them to help protect their sisters. So, naturally, I think of our house as the safest of safe spaces. Even with that, we didn't allow the girls to walk around with just their nightgowns on, without shorts or leggings underneath. We also kept them all from watching sexually charged TV shows and movies.

In the end, it didn't matter. Evil always seems to find a way in through generational curses, and it doesn't take a pastor or an evangelist to figure that out.

So much happened after that. I talked to my sister Krystal about what had been discovered, and she told me to reach out to that Dr. Robin (actually Robin Smith) from *The Oprah Winfrey Show*. Well, little did I know that once you do that, Child Protective Services is immediately contacted and suddenly knocking at your door.

My family was torn apart. The preditor was charged and was required to be separated from the home and put into a treatment center. My mother was angry at me because I spilled a family secret, and I was so confused and hurt because all I could think about was Kelsey and her rights as the victim and all of the times that I'd been abused and no one had cared enough to advocate for me.

We also sought therapy as a family, and boy was that a shit show. It caused my sisters and I to become estranged for some time, and I thought we would never recover. I think my sisters and I have put it behind us, but so many things have transpired over the years. And I was never fully able to trust any man or boy to be alone with my daughters again.

My youngest daughter, Raven, was also victimized. It happened when Angel, my third and current beau, reconciled with his eldest son, Tony, after years of being estranged. Angel's grandsons had been wanting to come over and hang out, and they finally spent the night.

As we were getting ready for bed, I asked, "Angel, what are the sleeping arrangements going to be?" Because I don't want my girls sleeping anywhere near the boys, since that's my safety zone, right?

"I think the boys should sleep up front," I said to Angel.

Against my better judgment, however, I decided to let it go so the arrangements weren't completely to my comfort level when Angel assured me it would be fine.

There we were, lying in bed. I don't think we were there 30 minutes when Angel got restless.

"My spirit is telling me something isn't right," he announced to me.

So, he went to sit on the living room couch when something compelled him to go to the front of the house. He peeked in on Raven and turned the light on. His grandson was there in her bed. Both of their pajama bottoms were down.

Raven was paralyzed, confused, embarrassed. She was only 14. The grandson was 15. I heard the commotion and ran up to the bedroom and went off. I started screaming at my daughter, thinking that maybe this was consensual.

"What the hell are you two doing?" I yelled, slapping Raven upside the head. "What the fuck are you doing? Have you lost your mind?"

Angel immediately swung into action and ordered to his grandson, "Get your clothes, get your shit, we're going NOW!"

But while this was all happening with the chaos and everything, I was in there talking to Raven, and she was confiding in me.

"Mommy, that's not all that happened," she said.

"What else happened?"

"He tried to go in me. I told him, 'Stop, that hurts.' He's saying, 'Relax, relax. It's gonna be fine.'"

When I heard that, I lost it. I knocked this boy upside the head and screamed, "Get him the FUCK out of here!"

Meanwhile, this kid was yelling back at his grandfather, being completely disrespectful.

"I didn't do anything! I didn't even touch her! You're choosing these people over your blood!" He's just regurgitating things he's heard his father say, right? It was horrible.

At this point, because my whole life has been about trying to protect my girls from this type of abuse, all bets were now off. I knew I needed to do something that was never done for my mom after she was abused, that was certainly never done for me. My mother warned, "You don't tell people about it."

When this happened to Kelsey, I was forced to reveal what happened. This time, it would be a conscious decision.

I'm telling, because it's the shame and the silence that perpetuates this across generations. What's wrong is wrong, and it needs to be taken out of the shadows and brought into the sunlight. There had to be a consequence, because that's the only way it could lead to therapy, healing, and education.

So, I asked Raven if she wanted me to call the police, if she wanted to go to the hospital, if she wanted to make a statement. She said she wanted me to contact the authorities. We phoned the police. I told Angel that he needed to give a statement. I could tell in that moment that he was hesitant—first of all, law enforcement coming into our home was not in his comfort zone. Ever.

I immediately came to a decision. You don't want your family hurt, but you've got to do what's right.

"Listen," I said to Angel, "I'm not asking you to choose me over your son or your grandson. But I'm telling you right now that I'm choosing my daughter. And if you don't agree to give a statement about what happened here, there's going to be a problem. We're over. We're done. Get the fuck out!"

Oh, he knew I was serious. Very serious. And he was incredibly offended. He's still broken up about it, because he feels like he failed to protect my daughter.

Angel made the statement. His son, meanwhile, was predictably defending his own son. He tried to make it appear that Raven was a willing participant. Angel said, "Listen, I don't care what he said, what she said. She was in her room in her bed. And he was in her room, in her bed. He had no right to step across that threshold. Period."

He added, "I don't care if she told him to come into her room and do whatever. He was older. He knew better. He knows we don't play that. It doesn't happen in our family."

Angel didn't have the history that I had with this. But I know that Tony's uncle, his mother's brother, sexually assaulted each one of his kids and is still in prison for it.

The bottom line is, hurt people usually hurt people. Abusers typically re-abuse. It's what they know. Boys especially tend to repeat the offenses. As parents, we always have to be hyper-aware. It can be a very tough world out there, with abusers abounding. We don't need to be bitter or cynical, just have our eyes open at all times.

10 CONTROL

LET ME BACK UP FOR a moment and tell you the story of exactly how I lost my virginity. As is already obvious, I grew up in a highly sexualized atmosphere. It started with my being molested quite a few times early on. Men and boys were always violating me, but I also experienced consensual encounters with a few girls. We're talking about a little bit of experimenting, playing around, kissing, touching, and feeling.

But there came a day when I was 14 and decided it was time to officially lose my virginity. In my mind, I said, "I don't want to be a virgin anymore," but I now know those thoughts came from being violated repeatedly. I didn't want someone to take it from me. I wanted to be the one in control of it.

I made the choice: It's going to happen today. I called up one of my male friends in the neighborhood. His name was Antonio, Tony for short.

"Hey," I said. "I want you to take my virginity today."

"Um, okay," he said.

"For real, we have to do it today."

"All right. For real, I'm down with it. Where we gonna do it?"

"Meet me at my grandfather's house tonight." I told him that I would leave the back door unlocked for him. See, I was living with my Poppy at the time, and he gave me a curfew that I kept violating by sneaking out the front door. So, he decided to sleep in the front room so that I couldn't sneak out, but

I guess he never thought that I would sneak out, or better yet sneak someone IN, the back door.

I heard the door open to the back porch, then I lifted the bedroom window to let him in directly to the bed I was sleeping in. That was it. We did it.

It wasn't really romantic or anything. What the hell did I know about romance? Shoot, I was 14, and I had an agenda, a goal in mind. When he was done, I told him to leave, and I remember him looking a little puzzled. Usually it was the guy who was hitting it and quitting it, but this time it was me!

I was taking control. The guy who took me for the first time was maybe 17 or 18. Honestly, I don't remember for sure. I'm surprised that I still remember his name.

Was this statutory rape in Washington, D.C., where we were? I couldn't even tell you. We also didn't use any protection. I could have gotten pregnant, I could have gotten a disease. Any number of things could have happened, but thank God, for once nothing did.

The most indelible memory of that day had nothing to do with the sexual experience itself. It was going into the bathroom right after, cleaning myself up, looking in the mirror, and rejoicing that I was no longer a virgin.

I said it out loud: "I'm not a virgin anymore, and I'm the one who made the decision!" And then I broke down in tears.

You have no idea how powerful it can feel for someone who has felt so little influence over her own sexuality to be the one who took the initiative to become the assertive one. That might have been a moment to celebrate had I been of age, and even though this impulsive act gave me back my power,

I have often wished I had a different story to tell as to how it happened. But what's done is done, and I was determined never to relinquish my power again.

11 OH MY GOD!

MY LIFE CHANGED AT 15.

I had just gone out and lost my virginity months before. But I found God soon thereafter and decided to give my life to Christ. My favorite uncle, Kirk, had been asking me to come to church, and I would do anything for him. I went and was compelled by the praise team (music was my passion) to go up and give my life to the Lord. Once I made that decision, I was instantly filled with God's spirit and began to speak in an unknown tongue.

This is why spirituality has been so real to me. I don't have a history of religiosity and belief. Since I didn't grow up in the church, I wasn't able to look at people and mimic them. I'd never seen it. I'd never heard it. I'd never experienced it.

Until I did.

Suddenly, I was doing this thing like I was possessed, and I couldn't explain it. I was overtaken by the Holy Spirit in a way I couldn't imitate. It wasn't my mind playing tricks on me. It was real.

It was like I was sold out for God for about a year. I was the girl in school talking about the Lord in class and holding Bible studies for a year straight. Then I got hooked up with my first love, Raoul, and I fell away.

But I remained a Christian, albeit a backslidden one. Fast forward, something happened early in my marriage to my second husband, David, that scared the crap out of me. David was at that time a practicing Muslim. He was involved in one faith, I was involved with another, so there was a lot of turmoil going on in the house and I believed a spiritual battle as well.

I was talking to David one day about the story of Job, and he was getting really angry because we weren't in a good place.

"Fuck it, man!" he yelled. "If God is real and all that stuff, then why are we going through what we're going through? Why are we struggling like this? Fuck God! I don't give a damn about God! Fuck God!"

I continued to tell David about Job. And as I did, I literally went into a panic. I couldn't breathe or speak. All the air just suddenly left my body. The words got stuck and wouldn't come out.

I still consider myself a spiritual person. I've seen people who were actually demon-possessed. I've watched people being taken through deliverance and having devils cast out. I've been a part of that. I believe it's genuine. And when I suffered that incident with David, I really feel like it was a spiritual attack, like the devil was just trying to shut me up. That scared me. A lot.

On top of that, I was having these recurring nightmares that felt like my soul was in limbo. This battle was between going back to church and living right, instead of doing everything under the sun. This battle came out in the most intense dreams imaginable, where people were dying all around me. There was death everywhere, blood pouring, and people that

I love being bludgeoned. This frightened me enough to run back to the church.

When I called the pastor of the church where I used to go and told him what had happened, he invited me to Bible study. This was Pastor Jeff. I went to his house, and he told me that my dreams were a test. In his view, it represented a journey out of the darkness and into the light.

While I was there and he was praying for me, he said that God had given him a vision.

"This vision is God telling me you are like a well," Pastor Jeff said, "the same way that people need to drink water from a well to survive. There's something about you when you walk into a room. People gravitate toward you. They draw from you. But when you fell away from God and started getting into all sorts of lasciviousness, God put a lid over that well, and as a result people can no longer draw from you."

Pastor Jeff concluded, "What God is showing me now is a struggle being waged for your soul. God is saying, 'It's now time for the lid to come off.'"

That was some powerful stuff.

Flash forward to 2010. I was having a serious conversation with my pastor and spiritual father, Peter. It was getting to the end of my marriage. I was no longer in love with David and had been wanting a divorce for some time, but David didn't want to go to counseling to discuss it. We'd already tried one session with Pastor Mark Carson of Refuge Living Sanctuary, a church we started attending when our previous church had fallen apart. David insisted, "I don't need somebody telling me what a bad husband I am."

David later admitted to me that the reason he didn't want to go to marriage counseling was because of his fear that I'd realize through the process that he wasn't the man for me. But that's another story for another time.

As time went on, a few years later, I was falling for another man. I confided this to Pastor Peter, who was for many years like a father to me. Peter was a guy who you either loved or you hated. He was very charismatic, had a strong personality, handsome, great wife, great kids, family man. But he rubbed some people the wrong way because he could be very stern and a little arrogant.

Whenever anyone said anything negative about Pastor Peter, however, I defended him. After relocating from Maryland to Dallas, Georgia, and then Dallas, Texas, my emotional affair with Angel Black, the former personal protection officer for gospel artist Greg Gammond, became physical. I also confided in him about my predicament, being pregnant with a child that wasn't my husband's. (I will give you the juicy details of how that all went down later.)

After I had a very difficult discussion with David regarding the situation and about Angel, David called up Peter, livid. He was angry that his spiritual father and pastor (David had since converted from being Muslim) hadn't told him about this, and Peter lied and told David he didn't know.

Now Peter was angry with *me*.

"You threw me under the bus with David!" he fumed.

"What do you mean?" I asked, incredulous.

"You told David that I knew about this!"

"Well, you did," I pointed out. "I didn't throw you under any bus. I didn't know you lied to him and told him you didn't know!"

I couldn't even believe I was having this conversation with a man I exalted above all others. But it was about to get worse.

"When was the last time you and David had sex?" Peter asked.

"I don't know, and it isn't relevant," I responded. "What does it matter?"

"Well," the pastor said, "you could show that this is David's child."

"No, I can't," I said. "For one thing, he had a vasectomy."

"Vasectomies have been reversed, and people have gotten pregnant," he said.

Peter wanted me to have this baby and raise it as David's child, without David knowing the truth. And I refused. I'm not such a cold person that I would do that to David. He had already been through enough, and I was not going to do that to the child, either. I also wasn't going to do that to Angel.

I honestly couldn't believe my ears, that this was even coming out of the mouth of a person I so revered as a man of God. For him to suggest this was a good idea made me instantly see him in a different light. Suddenly, it was no longer about the truth for him but about perception and appearances.

Then came the capper.

"If you don't do as I'm telling you," Peter threatened, "I'm going to disown you."

I refused to do it. And he did cut me off, for good.

We have not spoken since.

Peter and his wife, Esther, had for so long seen me as their daughter. Yet over one incident, they were both willing to cast me out, because I refused to lie about and mischaracterize something that would have been entirely wrong.

After this life-altering experience, my whole thing has become more about God symbolizing love and not this being that just wants to punish people. That's not my Christianity anymore. But I have to admit, this situation with Peter changed my view on so many things within the church. I just see things very differently today.

For instance, I used to be very hard on both of my sisters and my best friend, Sabrina, for all being lesbians—though I had had lesbian affairs myself—something that was strongly preached in the church as being immoral, something you would go to Hell for. All my ideals about those types of things are not the same as they once were.

The way I was ousted from the church gave me a lot to think about. My spiritual mother Esther was a package deal with my spiritual dad, and she gave me the love and support that my own mother had not. But that relationship was gone, too, in a heartbeat. When I needed her the most, I didn't have her.

But this said, I have certainly not removed God from my life. I strongly believe that God had me in a position where the reason I hadn't been severely hurt or killed in many very dicey situations was due to some sort of anointing that I'm walking in. I believe that God often uses me and speaks through me to help others.

People are drawn to me. There is a lot of chaos I'm attached to that has been a part of my life, but God always utilizes me for the betterment of the situation and having good come out of it. There are always lessons to be learned.

I don't believe that the fact my name, Angelia, means "Messenger of God" is an accident. I feel like, in many cases, I *am* His messenger. I'm sending messages. I'm receiving messages. I'm helping people through issues. I'm sometimes the sacrificial lamb. That doesn't always feel good, but the end result is typically positive.

Walking in the shoes that I walk in, I believe there is a certain amount of grace that covers me. It keeps me from being scared in difficult circumstances or getting caught up in drugs. Without the anointing, things turn out much differently.

But my experience with Pastor Jeff kind of changed the course of my life and probably saved it. It also (temporarily) saved my marriage. I was going to leave David, even so early on. Having the safety of the church covering me changed everything and made me live my life very differently.

The pastor said, "The Lord is telling me that you have much reserve and you're not going to run out." I took that to mean that God believed I would be able to get through whatever was happening and stick it out, that I would be strong enough to get through it, together with my husband.

The fact that David eventually gave his life to the Lord told me I'd made the right decision. Until it wasn't. He too turned out to be something and someone totally different than what he portrayed.

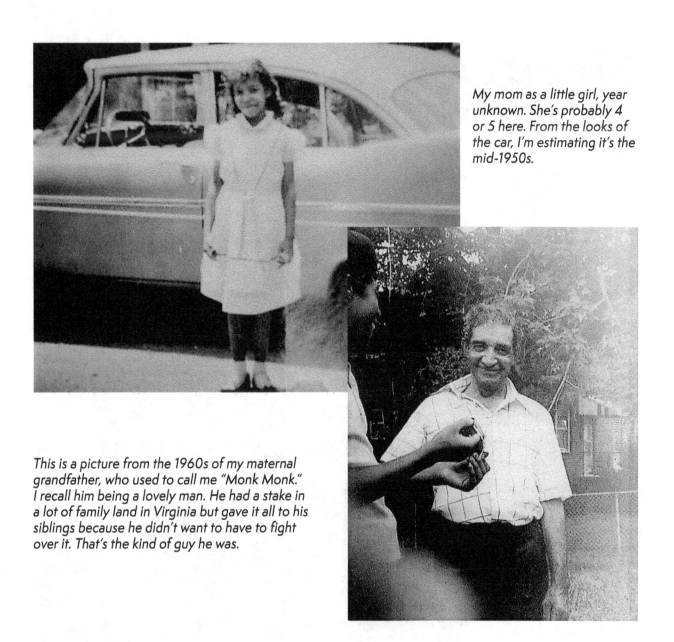

My mom as a little girl, year unknown. She's probably 4 or 5 here. From the looks of the car, I'm estimating it's the mid-1950s.

This is a picture from the 1960s of my maternal grandfather, who used to call me "Monk Monk." I recall him being a lovely man. He had a stake in a lot of family land in Virginia but gave it all to his siblings because he didn't want to have to fight over it. That's the kind of guy he was.

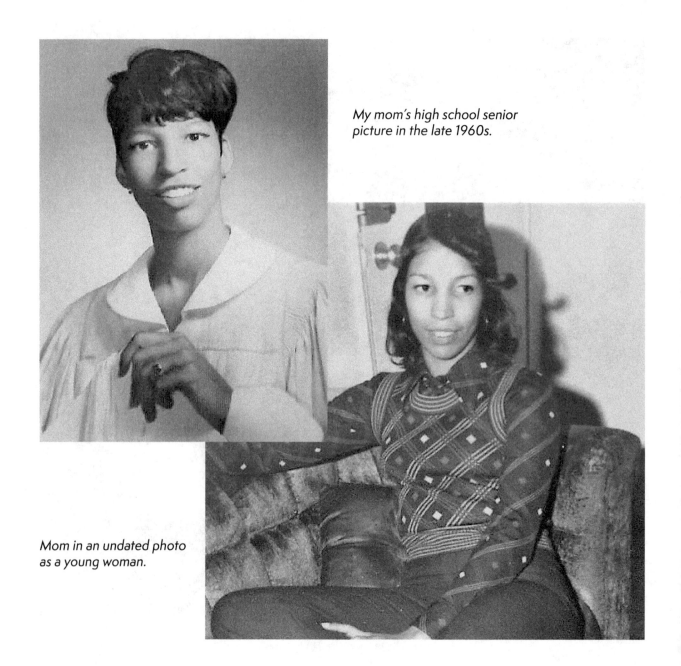

My mom's high school senior picture in the late 1960s.

Mom in an undated photo as a young woman.

Me and my older sister when we were little. I'm on the left, she's on the right. I'm either 3 or 4 here in the mid-1970s.

Me and my sisters. I'm on the far right. This was at our childhood family home in Bladensburg, MD. I'm 7 or 8 here.

Angelia Robinson

We're in my older sister's police cruiser. She was a Maryland State Trooper. I come from a family of law enforcement. That's me leaning on the front passenger window, my younger sister in the back and my older sister driving. It was the Eighties. I was a teenager.

Yes, I was a pompom girl at Central High in Capitol Heights, MD, in 1989. And let me tell you, we worked much harder than those damned cheerleaders. We did 12-minute routines that left girls passing out, vomiting, and needing oxygen.

Left: At my high school prom in 1990.

Below: This is me at either 18 or 19, a promotional photo for my fledgling music career right out of high school. I think we're talking 1991. It was shot on the waterfront in D.C., in Georgetown.

Me and my Ride or Die BFF, Brie Curtis. This was during my cabaret days around 1995, in Maryland.

Brie and me in 2018 at Koko's Pub in Baltimore. Still my Ride or Die, 23 years later.

This is me, probably in 1995, in D.C., with the flapper hairstyle.

Me and my brother Hakim, at a friend's house in D.C., around '96.

Left: My drug-dealer ex, Wayne, and my eldest son in '98.

Below: Me with my brilliant photographer friend Jackie Hicks, at her birthday celebration in 2004. She considers herself a portrait artist, and the amazing quality of her work shows it.

Who R U?

Me and the actor and comedian Anthony Anderson ("Blackish") in 2009 at the Gotham Comedy Club in New York City, where Anthony and a friend were hosting that night.

With Cathy Hughes, owner of the company Radio One and the One Love Gospel Cruise, at the 24th Annual Stellar Awards for gospel music in 2009.

With the great gospel artist Yolanda Adams at the Stellar Awards in 2009.

The cover of my CD, Lessons in Love, which dropped in 2009. (Photo credit: Jackie Hicks/Fond Memories Photography; Make-Up credit: Kym Lee)

Right: During the Lessons in Love *promotional photo shoot in 2009. (Credit: Jackie Hicks/Fond Memories Photography; Make-Up: Kym Lee)*

Left: During the Lessons in Love *photo shoot in 2009. (Credit: Jackie Hicks/Fond Memories Photography; Make-Up: Kym Lee)*

A 2009 promo poster for my Lessons in Love *CD.*

Who R U?

My father, Reds Bowman-Horton, and all his kids to mark his 60th birthday in 2009. Clockwise from top: Monique, Randy, Monica, Katisha, Roderick, and me. (Credit: Jackie Hicks/Fond Memories Photography)

Angelia Robinson

Me and my sister Katisha at our dad's 60th.

Who R U?

Signing a CD at a promo event for Lessons in Love *in 2010.*

Angelia Robinson

Singing at the promo event for Lessons in Love *in 2010.*

Left: This was taken on the day that Angel and I met on the One Love Gospel Cruise In 2010. It would take a while for us to get together for real, but it would be worth the wait.

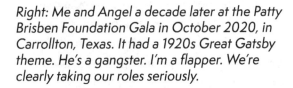

Right: Me and Angel a decade later at the Patty Brisben Foundation Gala in October 2020, in Carrollton, Texas. It had a 1920s Great Gatsby theme. He's a gangster. I'm a flapper. We're clearly taking our roles seriously.

12 THELMA & LOUISE

Yᴇᴀʜ, ᴍʏ ʙᴇsᴛɪᴇ Sᴀʙʀɪɴᴀ (Bʀɪᴇ) and I were like Thelma and Louise from the movie of the same name. Lots of guys. Plenty of adventures. A whole bunch of trouble. Sometimes things like my attachment to God got in the way, but we always wound up back together. Some relationships are just like that. I guess I'd call it destiny.

A lot of our connection when we were younger surrounded fighting and fun. We never fought each other, but let's just say Brie didn't mind throwing those hands. It started with her childhood gang affiliations. There was the M Team, Lady M Team, and the Baby M Team. That M stood for Mattapony, which was the name of the apartment complex that Brie grew up living in. She took no shit from anyone and didn't bother with trash talking. If you talked shit, she'd just pop you in the mouth.

But don't just take it from me. Listen to Brie tell it, too. Brie says:

> Our times growing up weren't always rock 'em, sock 'em, knock 'em out. Okay, maybe they were. I remember a time in middle school where Joan (your mother) thought I was a bad influence—which was totally false, because you were the wild one who would rebel and receive bad marks on your report card. Joan forbade you and me from talking on the phone and seeing each other. But you told your mom that I was an honor-roll student, and that shut down Joan's claims.

Yes, I was an A/B student. Our algebra teacher, Mr. Dooley, gave us a pop quiz one time, and you asked if I would allow you to cheat off me. I mean, you were the bestie. I couldn't let you receive a failing grade. So, I did, and you got an A while I received a B. How did that even happen? I was so upset!

I also remember about the music and how talented you were. You were always a great singer. You had stage presence. I could hold a note but couldn't compare to your pipes. I stayed in my lane as the lyricist (rapper) and your dancer. I was the best female pop locker and breakdancer in the school. No one could touch me!

Brie and I were inseparable. We met in the seventh grade at William Wirt Middle School. There were a lot of fun escapades in class. She was a jokester and very popular, and she always had my back. My front too.

There was a time when we lived together during high school. I was angry with my mother, as usual, and just wanted to get away. I fought with Brie's sister and brother over stuff, like my accusation that her brother Junior had stolen my then-very popular used jeans. Those jeans were the latest trend at the time and we wore them baggy, which is why he stole them. She wound up with a black eye from her brother, after confronting him on my behalf, and another time, a busted lip from her sister. Fighting was just a way of life in her family. And when I lived there, a lot of it was about defending me.

Brie turned me into a fighter, too, even though that wasn't really something I did nearly as instinctively as she did.

There was the one time where this girl named Dani had words with me over a Jamaican guy we apparently were both seeing, named Red. Dani's and my run-ins were coming to a head, and there was nothing like my bestie hyping me up.

It was an epic moment. We rolled up on the hood of a white Hyundai Elantra belonging to Brie's Aunt Boochie. Dani stood on the balcony running her mouth, and Brie started talking shit to the woman who was with her, instigating. Brie challenged the mouthy woman to come down and fight. As soon as she did, Brie just clocked her and then down came Dani running to jump in. It was ON!

Once Brie gave that woman a good old-fashioned ass-whupping, she became like a referee—"Get her, Angie, get her!"—and I was just swinging and swinging until I felt like I couldn't move my arms anymore. I was just so tired from knocking her upside her head. My final blow sent her running. Thank God!

The crazy stuff Brie and I did together almost always involved some drama. Like, there was the time in high school when Brie dated a big-time drug dealer. Meanwhile, I was dating his friend, who I knew was being unfaithful—so I got mad and keyed his car. He knew I had done it, and he pulled up on me to talk.

He was really calm.

"Did you key my car?" he asked.

"No," I lied, "why would I do that?"

He didn't have any interest in talking anymore after that. Instead, he put an arm around my neck, got me in a headlock, and started choking me. He choked me to the point of my nearly passing out. As tough as Brie was, it was hard for her to intervene, because this guy was not to be fucked with. So, she leaned to her then-boyfriend for assistance. She was begging him to make him stop. He finally did.

That would be the last car I ever keyed.

There was nothing that I noticed about Brie when we were in our teens growing up that would indicate she had an attraction to women. We both dated guys and had a whole bunch of crazy exploits with our male friends. We double-dated and had a great time. She wasn't at all interested in women romantically that I was aware of, until we got to be around

20, when she came out as a lesbian. When that happened, her sister blamed me for making her that way. As if you can turn someone gay!

Back when I had given my life to the Lord, at 15 years old, I called Brie up and told her we couldn't be friends anymore. Why? Because she wasn't saved, and I was. I was sold out for God and did what I believed I was supposed to do. We both cried. After that, she met a girl named Deborah, who became her new best friend.

The estrangement didn't last forever. But there were other times where we wound up hurt. For instance, she won tickets to go to Hawaii for free—and took Deborah, who was her "other" best friend at the time, instead of me.

Another time, I called into the radio station and won two tickets to see our favorite group New Edition. I called you after I'd won, and we were so excited. But the excitement died after a few days when Joan told you that you couldn't go. So, I took my friend Crystal. Sorry!

A bigger issue arose later in life when I told Brie at one point that I could never attend her wedding if she married a woman. This was a time when I was again heavily into the church and had these ideals, which included not supporting gay marriage.

"I couldn't witness you getting wed to another woman," I admitted. "I just couldn't support that lifestyle."

It turned out Brie was understandably really hurt by this. How hurt? Well, when she was planning to marry her current wife, she never told me about it. The conversation stuck with her, and even though I had long since changed my feelings on the issue, she somehow assumed I still felt that way.

This is how Brie remembered it:

When you told me yet again that your beliefs wouldn't allow you to attend or be in my wedding, I was devastated. I couldn't understand it, but my grandma told me not to question it. And I didn't. So when I was ready to marry my wife Nina, I called Krystal and Talia to extend the invite. I excluded you from the guest list. I carried that anger around until I couldn't any longer and we talked about it.

Your reasons didn't sit well with me. That's why we didn't speak for a while. Yes, I'm stubborn. Hell, I was in your wedding, but you robbed me of having my bestie in MY wedding!

As a result, I found out Brie had gotten married from a Facebook post. She hadn't invited me because she didn't want to get rejected by me all over again. That left me hurt, but I understood. This was maybe four years ago. We've since talked it out, and we're good now. But having to hear about it secondhand was hard. I'd be lying if I said it wasn't.

Today, Brie says:

I married my best friend! You and my wife Nina have the same birthday and share many of the same characteristics. Arrrrgh! A blessing and a curse. But hey, ups and downs, thick and thin, you're my bestie 'til the end! From the Wirt to the Dirt, I love you!

How are Brie and me today? Like nothing ever happened. She lives in Maryland with Nina. I live in Texas with Angel. If I called her right now and told her to get on a plane because I needed her, she'd come. The same applies to her if she called me. That's just how we roll.

I feel entirely blessed to have a friend as close as Brie. A lot of people go through their lives never experiencing that. Having her in my life is golden. We've survived the test of time. We always will.

Forever my Ride or Die!

13 IN DA CLUB

As I've already made clear, Brie and me went through a lot of escapades together. I mean a *lot*. But I also had another close girl-friend who I called my "other" best friend. Her name is Roachell. Nope, that's not a misprint, it's really spelled like that. Our most outrageous time had to be when someone was shot and killed right in our face, following a cabaret.

The thing used to be house parties. Then that turned into cabarets. Instead of going to the club, people would rent out an event center and you'd have a big cabaret. There we were, after leaving this cabaret, sitting in our car in the parking garage underneath the building, when we saw a guy running in front of us—and then we heard shots.

"Shit, that guy just got shot!" I screamed.

We freaked out! That could have been us!

I rolled down my window to better hear what was being said during this commotion, but I was so discombobulated. People were running and screaming everywhere. I think I was going into shock or whatever, and I didn't know what else to do. When someone gets gunned down right in front of you, it feels like you're in the middle of a movie. It doesn't seem real. And I guess not surprisingly, my brain stopped functioning properly.

There I was, reaching for the door handle and lock and everything, and for whatever reason, I couldn't figure out how to make them work. I eventually just climbed out of my driver's side window. It seems so crazy now that I could figure out how to roll down my window but couldn't unlock my door and get out. I guess that's what happens when you panic.

Roachell and I were finally out of the car. But instead of running for cover, we were standing there, stupid. Then we walked over and stood over this guy's dead body, just watching the blood continue to pour out of him.

I mean, it was the strangest and most surreal thing. Everything that was going on with the drug scene and the violence made this just suddenly seem completely normal. People were dying all over the place.

I was for some reason always drawn to the thug life, no matter how dangerous it was. Roachell was born and raised in the hood and had been shot once with a stray bullet in the chest, and almost died. She had her first child at 14 and was a fighter, too, just like Brie. She was a very pretty, chocolate girl who had curves in all the right places. She had a DONK! (That's Ebonics for Fat Ass) and all of the guys loved that.

Sadly, I'm the black girl who has no ass. I'm sure I could buy one now but I'm not DYING to get one.

Okay, I digress.

Roachell was the bestie who I got into trouble with as a young adult back in D.C., whereas Brie was the bestie who I got into trouble with as a young teen. I'm surprised I'm still alive or not up under a jail cell. Roachell taught me how to shoplift for designer handbags. She had great fashion sense and wore all designer clothes and accessories. She always had a friend who worked somewhere and could give us the "hook up" on clothes to wear to the club, because we could never wear the same clothes twice.

We went to the club every weekend. The Mirage was our club of choice for a long time, and then there was Tracks. We would stand outside in the cold, waiting in line just to get in and stand around and look pretty. I'm going to keep the rest of this kind of short, too, because if I let it, the number of fuck-ups I made would fill a book by itself. I make all the mistakes so you don't have to. Isn't that generous of me?

Here is one example:

One night at the Mirage, I ran into a guy who was drunk, talking a little vulgar, wanting to get my number. It's the kind of situation I've endured a hundred times before. I always tried to be patient and not be the snooty girl who would blow you off rudely. But this guy was persistent and simply would not take no for an answer. He just didn't like the fact I wouldn't give him my number.

So, he hit me. Punched me right in the jaw. I never saw it coming. Before I knew it, I was in a daze. The room was spinning. I was holding my head and lying on the ground. It was like the whole floor had parted, and now I was on the other side of the room from where I had been at the bar. Must have been a helluva punch.

"What happened, Angie? Are you okay?"

"Yeah. That guy just punched me in the face."

"What?"

"Yeah. Shoot, I can't focus."

My mistake was trying to reason with a drunk guy in the first place. I was there with Roachell of course, who was with a guy she was dating named Chuckie. Now, Chuckie was a very well-known guy not to fuck with, and he looked at me as his baby sister. And now Chuckie was looking for this guy who clocked me, searching for him all night. But I think as soon as the dude hit me, he must have high-tailed it out of the club.

It was a good thing for him that he left. Things would not have ended well for him if Chuckie and his boys had found him. But I never saw the guy again.

Drama like this always seemed to follow me. Someone for some reason wanted to fight me or hit me, dragging me into some kind of issue. Why? I couldn't figure it out, but Roachell—a dark-skinned woman—had a theory.

"There's this thing with light women and dark women/men, and this guy who hit you, he was a dark guy," she said. "You're light, and that seems to spark insecure feelings since the lighter women were more to be desired. So, darker guys always want to hurt or control you light women.

"The darker women are angry that you've got light skin and they don't. They also think you're weak, so they are always looking to try to hurt you, mess up your face, not thinking you can defend yourself."

Roachell said this was what she knew to be true from growing up in the hood. I think there may have been something to it. It's racism within your own race. It's stupid, you know? And it always surprised me when I wound up in the middle of some drama. Every. Single. Time.

14 I'M DOING ME

IT WAS IN THE SECOND grade that I discovered I had the gift to sing.

We had a talent show audition at Bladensburg Elementary in Maryland. I was determined to be in the show, and I wanted to dance. At home, I'd put these records on and do all kinds of elaborate dance moves, feeling pretty good about it.

But then I went to this audition and totally choked. I just stood there. The music was on, and I started moving left to right, left to right, and...nothing else. I totally froze. Age seven and washed up!

But the music teacher, Mrs. Vasquez, was amazing, and she saw something in me.

I loved Mrs. Vasquez. She was a very classy lady, tall and slim, and always wearing this beautiful red lipstick. Very fair, almost ghostly skin. Very dark hair. She wore these poodle-style skirts cinched at her waist with a big stylish belt. Every time she drank from her coffee cup, she'd leave a lipstick mark on it. I remember that very vividly, and I can't stop smiling as I write about her.

After I screwed up the audition, instead of saying, "You suck and you didn't make it," Mrs. Vasquez just pivoted to, "Angie, can't you sing? I remember hearing you in music class. You have a nice voice. You should sing for me."

I sang "Inseparable" by Natalie Cole for Mrs. Vasquez. And I made it into the talent show.

From that point on, all the way up until the sixth grade, Mrs. Vasquez put me into every talent show and cast me as the lead in every play. We did "Babes in Toyland" as the holiday play, and I learned to sing in French. I got popular, due to my voice.

By the sixth grade, I was using my falsetto voice a lot, and the teacher wanted me to project more. The thing is, I never had any type of vocal training. I don't think I really knew how to transition, or how to sound good singing full out. I kept trying to get louder and louder. Finally, I just copped an attitude and was like, "Well, I can't get any louder. If you want me to sing louder, you'll just have to find somebody else."

And Mrs. Vasquez did exactly that.

In other words, I got a big head. And it temporarily put me on the sideline. But I had a comeback and performed Diana Ross' "Mirror, Mirror" at the sixth-grade talent show.

I stayed connected to music after that by forming a singing group with my sister Krystal and one of her friends. We performed locally quite a bit, and I just knew I was gonna be famous. But then after high school, the Nineties started, and all the young girls were starting to hook up with rappers. Including me.

I remember this one concert I went to with Brie. It had MC Hammer, Digital Underground, Redhead Kingpin, all these other artists. Redhead Kingpin was fresh off doing the *Do the Right Thing* theme song in the Spike Lee movie of the same name. Brie had met this guy named Hakim and his friend Don. They were part of Redhead Kingpin's entourage.

My initial meeting with Hakim was supposed to be a hookup. But when we met each other, we didn't hit it off like that. We were just cool. "Oh, he's a college guy." "Oh, she's a cool girl." Like brother and sister from the get-go. So, we never slept together, which is why we've stayed great friends to this day.

Actually, I consider him to be my brother, and he considers me his sister. We love each other like crazy, and Hakim has always been the one constant man in my life who has never judged me and has been there for me, no matter what.

But Hakim did help me to hook up with Redhead Kingpin. I started hanging out with Kingpin, and we had a couple of rendezvous together. He took me to the Loop Inn Motel in Avenel, New Jersey, the first time I went to visit him. It was just sex. I later found out that he had a girlfriend. But he was a rap star at the time, so that was enough. It's crazy the stuff you do when you're young. And dumb.

Anyway, I traveled back and forth to New York in '90 and '91 with Hakim, and spent many nights there with him and his family. They came to love me and I came to love them. We recorded some singles, which were really big back then. If you didn't have a label, you'd do singles and EPs. It was the era right before Mary J. Blige hit, so it was really popular for R&B artists to sing over beats.

I was putting out these recordings and doing live performances at clubs and stuff. I wrote a bunch of songs and started to rap, too. My rapper name was Eboni Red, because I was a black girl but also red-boned.

But I ultimately drifted away from music to pursue other stuff. Men!!! More drug dealers!!! I couldn't get enough of that life. Stupid shit! I coulda been Mary J. Blige!

15 PAPA DON'T PREACH

So, as you recall, it turns out my sisters Krystal and Talia and I all had different dads, and mine was Randolph "Reds" Bowman Horton. How did he get so many names? Allow me to explain.

He got Randolph from his parents, along with Bowman. He was "Reds" because he has red hair and freckles, somewhat unusual for a black man. The "Horton" part came from marrying a woman named Cathy, whose family ran R.N. Horton Company Morticians, Inc., and also was the adopted daughter of the founder. It was the first black-owned funeral home in the Washington, D.C., area. Their slogan: "Service With Dignity at Any Cost."

My father ultimately came to be part owner. His wife, Cathy, was lazy and a drug addict for many years, and would have run the place into the ground or sold it had my dad not intervened and taken over. She is part owner really in name only. I guess her dad didn't want to completely cut her out.

Also, Cathy's father had two adopted sons, one who devastatingly died at three years old and another who also died a tragic death. I don't have much detail on that, but as a result, my dad took on her last name so Horton would live on. He also fathered five more kids after he split from my mother: Monica, Monique, Roderick, Randy, and Katisha.

Reds did well by marrying into the Horton Funeral Service family. He's a wonderful, popular guy. He used to play basketball, and he probably would have gone pro had he not gotten injured. That's the truth. He still is phenomenal on the court even in his seventies. My dad is very confident and often brags on himself, but I thought he was all talk at times. That quickly changed the day I went to watch him play, and I heard little kids whispering, "That's Reds, that's Reds, he's a legend."

Anyway, he and my mother divorced when I was two. But I didn't realize this until many years later. I honestly don't have memories of my dad until my pre-teenage years, although I was told that he was very much a part of our lives when I was younger. My stepdad Tim raised me as his own. I even vaguely recall my dad giving up his rights to me in court. I believe it was over child support. Doing that stopped it.

Then came the day we had a young girl visit us. Her name was Arnelda, and she was introduced to me as a cousin. My older sister Krystal, who's like a sister-mom with how she takes care of me, seemed to be favoring this girl, and everyone was being really nice to her. I got jealous over it, and then during an argument Arnelda just blurted out, "That's why Krystal is my sister!"

This was especially weird, because being my sister's sister would make her my half-sister, too, or so I thought until I was given all of the details. The thing is, I wasn't supposed to know this, but the girl just kind of tossed it out there as a vindictive declaration. I knew there

was no reason for her to lie, so I got incredibly angry. Once she said it, she had to leave and go home that same day.

That was the moment I discovered that Krystal and I also had different dads. And as I said, my own dad had a whole other family, another wife, and a bunch of kids, and they lived in a great big mansion. I became very angry, rebellious, and I didn't want to live at home with my mom and stepdad anymore. I asked to start seeing MY dad, and I remember my mom being very agitated. She said she didn't understand why I wanted to go see this man who wasn't taking care of me or wanting to spend time with me.

Mom told me the story of how when the judge ruled for child support, Cathy, my dad's wife at the time, had reported his salary as being especially low in an effort to make his child support payments equally low. Well, it worked. I believe it was only $250 a month that he paid in support of me, and those payments were not sent regularly. I didn't care! I loved my dad—or, well, I wanted to love him and get to know him. I started to go visit him and stay at his house sometimes, and it was all very eye-opening.

By the time I was in eighth grade, I was determined to live with Reds and Cathy and do my own thing. I was 12, and I wanted to date boys, and I couldn't do that with Mom, so I started playing things between the two parents. With Dad, it seemed much more likely I'd be able to have my way and a less strict atmosphere. Plus, we got driven to school in limousines and stuff like that. What was not to love?

Reds wasn't always a fine, upstanding guy, as I'll explain here in a second. But he became a responsible and respected businessman who did right by the funeral home. He built the place up while his wife showed up at the office and slept on the couch all day.

But let's discuss a different side of my father here for a second. Upon his divorce from Cathy, he had shared custody of their children. My dad moved from the mansion that belonged to Mr. Horton and into a row house (also owned by Mr. Horton) in uptown, NW D.C., with my siblings. Monica and Monique spent most of their time in boarding school. The boys stayed local. After putting the music on pause and moving from pillar to post, I decided to move in with Dad for a while.

He started waking me up early in the morning with complaints that this person and that person didn't show up for work at his car wash. See, my dad is a BOSS. He is the consummate businessman. I'm sure I get my business savvy from him. The car wash belonged to the funeral home. It was really smart to have it adjacent to the business so that all of the hearses and such could be cleaned on a regular basis with no outside costs.

Anyway, I needed the money, and he needed the help, so I started working there. At some point, he started sleeping with one of my friends, Ramona. That came as a surprise to me, but the bigger shock was that Ramona was a drug addict. That would soon be revealed after I came to meet the man who would end up becoming my first husband. My father didn't condone this relationship. Yet he called me in the middle of the night to have me ask my new boyfriend, Wayne, if he could buy some coke, which my man was selling at the time.

Yes, this was all just a little awkward.

Reds obviously had a past. He used to be a drug dealer himself. Then he opened up his own convenience store and got out of the drug game.

One morning when I was 19, I was asleep in my dad's house and I heard somebody banging on the front door.

"Let me in! Let me in!" It was a woman's voice, and she was yelling.

It was Cathy, my father's now ex-wife. They had four kids together, and Dad was living in a house that her father owned. She made me take the chain off the door and immediately ran upstairs and shoved her way into his bedroom.

"Angie, you see this? You see what your father's doing?"

On the dresser, I saw two glasses with foil on top of them and a single hole poked through. As I soon learned, this is apparently how you smoke crack. Oh, I should also mention that my father was at that moment in bed with a woman who looked to be a crackhead, this incredibly malnourished-looking black woman with very short hair and not at all attractive.

But at this point in my life, I didn't care what anyone said about him. I was all just about having my father's love. So, I shook it off like it was nothing. Never batted an eye. Never questioned him about it. Never judged him for it.

Fast forward more than two decades to the time when I decided to leave David. I'd been having an emotional affair with Angel. He made me happy in ways I had never felt before, and David and I needed therapy, of which he would constantly refuse. I eventually made the decision to leave David to be with Angel, and I soon thereafter became pregnant with Angel's child. When I told my father about splitting from David, he talked to me about the importance of working to keep the family together.

"Dad," I told him, "I've been barely existing in this marriage for many, many years, mostly just trying to be there for the kids. And it's getting volatile now. I don't think it's good for the children to try to stick it out."

Soon after that, I needed my father's help financially. I'd been calling him and calling him, and I always just got his voicemail. He was never available. It started to feel like he was avoiding me. Finally, Monique confirmed that he had just stopped speaking with me ("ghosting" is the term today) because he wasn't happy with the decision I'd made to leave David. He refused to take my calls without explaining why.

Like this man should judge!

Meanwhile, I'm sure Reds was getting an earful from David, because my husband was still in Georgia after I'd moved to Texas to work with Greg Gammond. But this not speaking to me thing just broke my heart. I don't know if I'd ever felt like that before. I couldn't believe he was siding with my ex and abandoning ME, his own flesh and blood. It hurt like hell!

Here I was, feeling especially emotional because of my pregnancy hormones. My mom had never had my back on anything. Now, my dad wasn't talking to me. I'm somebody who needs closure. I do okay if I can have that. But if you just drop off the face of the earth and don't tell me what I did, I don't do well with that.

This was my father, the one whose back I had no matter what he did or what anyone had to say. I was always defending him as a child, even against my own mother. I never judged him. So, for him to do me like that—it was the biggest betrayal. And I was broken. I even had suicidal thoughts.

It reminded me of what it was once like being the girl of a drug dealer.

16 MY JAMAICAN GUY

I WAS THE SUBURBAN GIRL who went to the hood searching in all the wrong places for love. I liked those bad boys. Don't know what that was all about, but I dated a lot of drug dealers. On so many levels, it's a miracle that I'm still around to write this book.

The guys who had the money and did the drug dealing, they were horrible partners. Big surprise, right? But for a time, it was very alluring, especially for black women like me who loved the thrill of being with guys who would treat them to a lavish lifestyle and could buy us stuff that our parents couldn't or wouldn't. You know what I'm talking about: the designer bags, the trips, the cars, the cash. That was the materialistic lure of the drug era.

It had nothing to do with the drugs themselves. As I've already said, I never tried drugs back then. Not a line of coke. Not a hit on a crack pipe. Not a pill. Nothing. Never even smoked weed.

I was good in school. I graduated high school at 17. But I was dumb in love. I guess it speaks volumes that I never actually knew the real name of my first husband until we were no longer together. He had several different aliases, but I called him Wayne. We hooked up when I was 18 and ultimately got married in the basement of the Upper Marlboro County Jail. I still can't believe they allowed it. That moment was so creepy when I think back on it. See, Wayne went to prison for dealing shortly after I had our son Franklin, and I reluctantly got hitched to him when I was 21, to keep him in the country. He was an illegal and was about to be deported.

We had gone through so much with all of his cheating and carrying on that by the time we married, I didn't even want to be with him anymore. I originally wanted to marry him for love, but when it actually happened it was more for convenience and to help him out. I'd already had a child by him, so I thought marrying him was the right thing to do. Of course, it wasn't.

But let me back up.

I met Wayne shortly after I moved in with my dad and started working at the car wash in D.C. Wayne came up to the window to pay for his car, and he had on this Maryland Terps sweatshirt.

"Hey, that's a nice shirt you're wearing," I said. "Are you going to buy me one just like it?" You know, just flirting. But Wayne took the bait.

"When do you want to go get it?" he asked.

"Well, I get off work at five."

And he actually came back at five, met me there, picked me up, and took me shopping at the store. That was the big thing back then with drug dealers, is you took your girl shopping, got her a designer bag, the jewelry, the necklaces, the swag.

What I didn't have in high school that many of the other girls got because I wasn't the *IT girl*, I was now getting. I was transforming, and it felt really good. I started looking a certain way. I fit that mold and became part of that world. I liked looking like money.

When Wayne and I got together, he was living in an efficiency, a one-room apartment. I could come and go to his place and go inside, but then that changed. We pulled up to his place one day and this woman came out and was ready to attack me.

"Who are you? Who are you?" she demanded to know in a threatening manner and with a Jamaican accent.

"I'm just a friend . . ."

She interrupted, "You're the one that my man's always coming home smelling like, that perfume, and then he don't have no nature for me!"

Saying he "don't have no nature for me" meant he didn't want to have sex with her. I had no idea who this woman was, and quite frankly, I didn't want to know, but I realized that whatever illusion I was under about being his only girlfriend was exactly that—an illusion.

Wayne got out of the car and said to her, "Go back in the house!! Cool now, man!!" He was speaking in Patois.

But after that, this same girl and a couple of her Jamaican friends came looking for me at my dad's car wash repeatedly, like stalking me. They probably wanted to beat my ass. But every time they came, I wasn't there, thank God. They arrived carrying machetes and whatnot.

You'd think Wayne might have told them to lay off me. Maybe he did. But probably not.

It wasn't until later that I discovered that, before he met me, Wayne had sent for his child's mother from Jamaica, this woman who met me at his apartment. They had a daughter together who I knew nothing about. Then he got caught up in his relationship with me. It was always a big thing for guys like him to take up with an American girl.

Things got really hostile with his other lady, and Wayne was always having to take me to a hotel. Eventually Maxine (that was her name) just disappeared and was no longer around, and he and I got our own place together. I later found out he'd moved her to New York.

I don't know why I expected that being the girl of a major drug dealer would be a smooth ride. What the hell was I thinking? What I quickly learned was that you didn't question most of what you encountered in the drug world. I'm too nosy, demanding, and controlling for that, though. There were a lot of things they were doing that you were not necessarily supposed to know about. But I could always tell it was something. Call it women's intuition.

How did I ultimately find all this stuff out? Well, after Wayne got locked up on another drug charge, I found out he had been going to this apartment and having his drugs sent there. He started staying there sometimes and got busted. After I received that call, the one that no drug dealer's wife or girl wants to get, I went to the apartment to get his things and found an undeveloped roll of film on a counter. This was back in the era before digital cameras, when you had to actually take film in and get it developed.

So, I developed this film and there were pictures of him and Maxine and the daughter, a dog, all of this stuff. He'd been keeping them over there, keeping me over here, having his cake and eating it, too.

I'd already had my suspicions, though. Before he got locked up, Maxine was trying to make me jealous, so she called me up to say, "Wayne just left my house."

"You're lying!" I shot back.

"I can tell you what he's wearing," she insisted. "He's got on a turquoise blue short set."

Wayne walked in the door, and that's exactly what the fuck he was wearing. He tried to deny he'd been over there, and I was like, "How are you going to explain this? She just told me you were there and what you were wearing, and you're wearing it!"

We got into this shouting match, and I jumped up and got in his face. I know I shouldn't defend this, but I think it was more like a reflex when he hit me. I guess he was trying to defend himself. I wound up needing stitches. As soon as he did it, he freaked.

"Oh my God! Oh my God! Angie!" he said in his deep Jamaican accent.

He jumped off the balcony of our apartment and split. Meanwhile, I had this gouge in my head, and it was pouring blood. I called my sister and my mother. They came over and were livid, even though I told them it was an accident, that he didn't mean to do it. They weren't buying it. They drove me to the hospital, and I got stitched up.

That wasn't the only serious trauma to come out of my time with Wayne.

During the moment when things were out of control and he was cheating on me right and left, I swallowed a bottle of pills. I don't even remember what kind of pills they were, to be perfectly honest. Must have been Tylenol or something. I called my sister Krystal, crying.

"Krystal. I just took a bunch of pills. I want to die."

"Shit! I'm on my way!"

I didn't really want to die. It was just a cry for help. I wanted Wayne to stop doing what he was doing, but that was never going to happen.

Anyway, it was just tearing me apart because I was so in love with this guy. He was like my sugar daddy. I guess I should have mentioned he was 19 years older than me—pretty much twice my age—when we met.

Krystal rushed me to the hospital. They wanted to pump my stomach, and even in the middle of my medical crisis, I was like, "Nope. Not doing that." So, they had me drink this black tar stuff that coats all the medication and helps you to pass it all through your bowels. They also kept me two days for psychiatric evaluation.

I don't recall having a lot of lingering damage from the suicide attempt itself. The most traumatic thing was going through a relationship with Wayne! I just wanted him to stop dealing and stop cheating but he wouldn't. It was who he was. What the hell did I expect?

Being with Wayne was pretty much one crazy distressing situation after another. And none was crazier than the time I caught him with some chick at a hotel.

Pull up a chair. This one's going to take a little while, but I promise that it's totally worth it.

I was 19 and looking to get back into music. I had settled down with Wayne and was ready to focus on it again. Krystal was managing me at the time. I was doing these little shows and things, as well as some traveling. Wayne and I had moved into our own place, and you may remember they had these answering machines with little tapes in the early Nineties. You could leave really long messages on them and record anything you wanted to, right?

Well, back when I was living with my dad, my little brother Randy, who was really handsome back then, with lots of female attention, was always sneaking into my room and talking to his friends. Fast forward to when Wayne and I were living together. While I was out of town one time, Wayne played a message on my answering machine and heard male and female voices. The girl wasn't really even talking. There was just a lot of giggling. The guy was asking if she loved him. The girl giggled and squealed, "Yeaaaaah."

Apparently, Wayne thought that the girl was me. He played it for my mother, who for some reason couldn't tell it *wasn't me*. What she should have said was, "Oh, no, that's not Angie. That's not my daughter." But of course, she didn't, because this was my mother. Instead, she just kind of cosigned that her daughter was doing something foul on her man.

Now Wayne was totally convinced I was cheating on him. So, what does he do? He took all of my performance dresses and ripped them to shreds. He set fire to pictures of me

posing with other artists like MC Hammer. I was just stunned.

My mother said, "Wayne thinks you've been cheating on him."

"What? Why? How?"

"Well, he found these messages on your answering machine, and he played them for me."

Now I was the one who was livid!!

"And you couldn't tell the voice on the recording wasn't me?"

"No, I honestly couldn't tell."

I played it for Krystal, and she immediately knew it wasn't me. But that's Mama. Throwing me under the bus at every opportunity.

Now, I was distraught. Tears were coming. I was blowing Wayne's phone up, but he wouldn't answer. He destroyed my things and took all the money out of the house. I didn't even have my car. He took that, too!

I started calling up this hotel that he and I used to go to before we got our own place. It was the Hampshire Inn. I could never forget it. We spent many nights there. I asked for his room. They rang a room. No answer. But I was stuck without wheels or cash. All I had was the bicycle. Good enough. I jumped on the bike and rode to Langley Park, Maryland, all the way from Hyattsville.

I got there, all sweaty and out of breath. But of course, the front desk wouldn't tell me the room number. Now I turned into the crazy lady who was banging on everyone's door to see which one he was in. People were coming out all nosy because they knew what was about to go down.

Finally, I got the right door. Wayne pulled the curtain to the side to see if it was me.

"Angie, whata gwan?! Cool now, man! Bumba Ras Claat!"

"No! The question is what are YOU doing? I know she's in there with you. Let me in there!"

"Angie, cool now, man . . . cool now, man."

"Don't you fucking tell me to calm the fuck down! Let me in!"

The one thing I knew was that Wayne loved this bike. It was a Cannondale. Very expensive.

"I will take this bike and throw it through this fucking window unless you open this door right the fuck now!"

He opened the door and continued to tell me to "cool down." Of course, there's a girl in there. What else would he be doing in a hotel room? I tried to get to her and he kept getting in my way, coming between us so I didn't pounce on her ass. She finally got away through the room door and rushed over to the adjacent IHOP.

I followed her over to the IHOP, walking up and down the aisles in the restaurant, flailing around, my hair all over my head, still sweating from the bike ride, totally looking like a crazy woman. I searched the bathroom. Nothing. She'd gotten away, and I was *pissed*! I never found her.

Then of course, I put the bike in his car and rode home with Wayne—and I was furious. I sat in the backseat and punched him in the head all the way home. He kept telling me, "You're the cheater, man. You cheated on me first."

"No, I did not!" I insisted. "That was my little brother Randy and some little girlfriend."

"No man, that was no Randy-sized voice."

"Yes, it was! Don't you know that messages stay on a tape for a long time? That was my little brother using my phone!"

But it was no use. There was no convincing him. And this began the downward spiraling of our relationship. I knew he was a cheater before, but this incident just made him more reckless.

Cut ahead now a little while. Our son Franklin was six weeks old, and I was driving around looking for Wayne. There were certain areas where the drug guys hung out, and I knew if I went there, I'd probably find him. But I found more than I bargained for. I spotted our Nissan Pathfinder. As I pulled up to the stoplight, I saw that it was definitely Wayne's truck. And who did he have in the passenger seat but a girl named Paula, who was supposed to just be someone who helped him package his drugs. She also lived in our neighborhood. How stupid was I back then?!

They saw me and took off. And I took off driving beside them, full speed ahead! When I tell you I know how to drive, I know how to drive. I had a six-week-old baby in the back, but in that moment I didn't think about that. I just saw red. When I'm determined, I can drive like Mario Fucking Andretti. That's just what I was doing. I cut corners. I screeched through alleys. I floored the damn thing.

Wayne could see that he wasn't going to lose me, so finally he pulled off into a gas station and let Paula out of the car. I stopped my own car and rushed out, even though my baby was still there strapped into the car seat. I ran over and tried to grab Wayne in the Pathfinder, but he bolted.

Well, guess who was still left there in the lot? Paula. She was the one I wanted, anyway. I proceeded to whoop her ass. I was punching her everywhere, all over her face and body, raining punches down as she screamed and tried to cover up. I was just whaling on this woman. It was so bad that some guys pulled into the gas station and dragged me off her.

"Enough," one of them said. "You've done enough. You've whooped her enough."

You know what they say about crimes of passion being real? Well, that's what this was. I didn't put Paula in the hospital or anything, but I was just on automatic. My fists had a mind of their own. If I'd had a knife or a gun in that moment, I'd have used it. Thankfully, I didn't.

It was relatively soon thereafter that Wayne was arrested and needed me to get him out of jail. I questioned whether I should do it, but wouldn't you know, I gave in again. I loved the guy. So, I wanted to get him out. I had to pay for an immigration lawyer because he was a Jamaican citizen. At this time, I was working at the Recording Industry Association of America (RIAA) in D.C.

I got him out of the Big House. I married him, reluctantly. And he wound up getting deported anyway. But he always managed to get back into the country.

Now, here I was, a single mother with a one-year-old son. I was maturing as a woman. I wasn't interested in that drug life anymore. That's when I told Wayne I didn't want to be with him.

"When you met me, this is what I was doing, and you didn't seem to mind then," he reasoned.

"Yeah, well, I didn't have a child then, and I have to think of him," I told him. "I really don't want this life anymore."

Wayne continued to do it. I mean, what else was the man going to do, become a college professor? But I had moved out of the apartment we shared and into my dad's basement in D.C., which I paid to have remodeled for my comfort. When Wayne came back from Jamaica, he asked my father if he could stay there, too. We were still married, after all. Reds was okay with it because Wayne promised to stop dealing.

Well, of course, he kept dealing drugs. Finally, I confronted my father.

"Dad, Wayne won't stop dealing. I want him out."

So, my dad did put him out. I eventually moved out and back to Maryland. I got my own place again. Gosh, I have moved so many times in my life it's ridiculous. Although I didn't want to be with Wayne anymore, there were still some things I needed from him. Sex and money. Wayne was great in bed, and heck, we were still married, so why not? He looked very different though. He had put on quite a few pounds, and it didn't look good on him.

Still, I convinced him to come stay with me at the new place, simply for a little companionship and so he would pay the bills. After all he had put me through, I thought it was the least he could do. But after a while, I just wasn't feeling it anymore. He was up to the same things.

I'd moved on mentally, emotionally, and physically, too. I didn't really want him to be around anymore.

One day, I finally just said, "I'm done." He came back to the house, but I'd changed the locks. He tried to get in and I was like, "Nope. Not letting you in."

"But Angie . . ."

He would "But Angie" me for the last time. "Nope. We're over."

I filed for divorce a mere thirty days before I was scheduled to marry my second husband, David. I had to rush this paperwork to the judge and get him to sign off on it so I could legitimately marry D. And I made it. Barely.

David never knew how close I was to my divorce not being final before marrying him. I never told him.

I wish I could say that was the end of Wayne for good. But that's never the way it works with drug kingpins.

A few years down the road, I was married to David, we already had our first child together, DJ, and I was pregnant with our daughter Kelsey. Wayne's mother (Franklin's grandmother, Myrtle McMain) was coming from Miami to see Wayne.

One day, I got this call from Myrtle: "Angie, as you know, I'm supposed to be coming to see Wayne. I have this plane ticket. But I haven't heard from him in two days. Have you heard from him?"

"No," I admitted, "I haven't heard from him, either."

"I don't know what to do. Should I still come?"

"Yeah, just come anyway," I said. "If you don't hear from him, I'll come pick you up from the airport."

That's just what happened. Wayne was out of contact, so I went to get Myrtle. And as she was approaching me at the airport, the FBI came out from everywhere with their guns drawn. Everything went into slow motion. What I didn't know was that they had Wayne in custody. I was able to play it cool, though. I mean, I had nothing to hide anymore. I was no longer with the man.

As soon as I laid eyes on Myrtle, the FBI stepped in and immediately separated us. They started showing me pictures and questioning me.

"Do you know who this is?"

"Yes. That's my ex-husband."

"Why are you here?"

"I'm picking up his mother from the airport."

"Why are you picking up a woman who is no longer your mother-in-law?"

"She's the grandmother of my son. I'm re-married and have another family."

"Well, who is this kid right here?"

"It's my son."

"And what is your relationship to the mother of the guy in custody?"

"I already told you. She's this boy's grandma. She's here visiting her grandson."

"Well, her son is in custody. Why did she come anyway?"

"Because she is here to visit her grandson."

On and on the questions went. My whole point was that I didn't know what was going on with Wayne, but I had nothing to do with what-ever it was he had done. They had nothing on Myrtle or me, so they had to let us go.

The feds hadn't let Wayne make a phone call because they thought they were going to have this big bust go down. But since they wound up with nothing, they had to allow him the call. The next day, he called me.

"Angie," Wayne said, "I'm locked up."

"Yes," I said, "I know."

"Okay, look, I need you to do me a favor. I need you to go to my apartment."

"What? I'm not your woman anymore and certainly not your errand girl. Why would I want to risk my ass while the feds have you in custody?"

This was the truth. He was no longer my man. I was in a whole other marriage. But he was begging me.

"Look, just please do this."

I was worried the FBI might be listening, but I went anyway.

"Go to the apartment," he said, "and look under the carpet in the usual spot." (This was where he always hid his money and I guess still did.)

Wayne continued. "I threw the keys out the back of the apartment, go look for them."

Well, I thought I could use some of this money too, as I was in the process of buying my first home and Wayne didn't help me financially to take care of our son. So, I had my own motive for wanting this to happen, besides helping Wayne.

Myrtle went with me to the apartment to look for the keys. I didn't find them. What did I do? The next best thing: I called a locksmith and had them come over to let me in the place. But as I was waiting outside and the locksmith was trying to jimmy the door, none other than my old pal Paula (Wayne's girlfriend now) showed up (she tended to show up a lot). I guess he didn't want to leave anything to chance in case I didn't come through.

Now Paula was there, and she had a motive because she knew there was money inside and wanted to get her hands on some for herself, from the Bank of Wayne (otherwise known as the spot beneath the carpet).

As soon as the guy got the apartment door open, Paula rushed in. I tried to rush too, but I was five months pregnant! Despite this fact, I got into a tussle with her, while Wayne's mother tried to talk sense to her.

"Stop it!" Myrtle screamed at her. "Don't you see? She's pregnant, leave her alone!"

Now, here came Paula's brother as another voice of reason. Suddenly, it was a family affair. The brother said, "Listen, Paula, don't do this. If Wayne wants you to have anything, he'll make sure that you get it. This is the man's mother. She's here doing what he asked her to do. You should not be involved here, and you need to leave."

This is not to say that Paula didn't grab some of the money for herself. She took a few handfuls and hid it under her clothes. I took the rest of the money from under the carpet, and it came to about $75,000. His mother had come from Miami in the first place because Wayne was about to move back to Jamaica and was trying to get out of the drug game. This was his seed money to launch his new, clean life.

It turns out he had withdrawn money out of *my* mother's bank account. Yes, you read right: MY mother. She loved Wayne and still helped him whenever she could, even though her daughter (me) was no longer involved with him.

Now let this all sink in for a moment. Here I had to fight with Wayne every month to get $225 in child support for the son we created together. Yet my very own mother was holding on to this very large sum of money for him and never said a thing. Plus, if she ever needed something, he would give her the money for it. I never had the first clue that they had this relationship. Whenever there was an issue between me and Wayne, my mother would side with the drug kingpin over her daughter because it was beneficial to her.

And people wonder why I might have a problem or two with the woman.

Anyway, I helped Wayne's mom get all his things packed up and shipped off to her in Miami so she could send it back to Jamaica. Wayne did wind up moving back to Jamaica, all right. He left Paula (who was pregnant) behind. Karma is a bitch, isn't it? His mom gave me $10,000 of the $75,000 that was under the carpet. Wayne begged me to give it back. But there was no way I would. That money was rightly mine to help take care of our son. He also begged me to give his car that was left behind to Paula, because she was pregnant—which I did.

The $10K came in handy. I used it for a down payment on our new house.

Postscript: I found out that Maxine, the mother of Wayne's other daughter, died in a car wreck a few years after Wayne and I split up.

After Wayne moved back to Jamaica, I heard he was just working in a hotel. But he had a lot of sins to atone for, and there was no telling what he had been involved with in his home country before. The word I got was that he got set up. He was out on a date with a girl and returned where he lived. He had to get out of his car to open the gate and pull into his driveway, and right then someone shot him in the head.

The strange thing was, he supposedly didn't know he'd been shot. He was just like, "Oh, somebody hit me in the head." He suddenly felt pressure, apparently. But as he's starting to lose consciousness, he was calling out for his father, and asking people to call his dad. He was alive for a few weeks, but then they took him off life support.

A predictably tragic end.

17 STAYIN' ALIVE

I'VE LOST A LOT OF friends to murder. Way more than I've lost to drugs. I guess I'm supposed to be here, because there sure were times I should have been in a place where people were killed—and if I *had* been there, I would've been dead right along with them.

Little things happened that made me decide not to be there. I feel like it was the hand of God, or whatever you want to call fate.

My habits, my movements, indicated I should have been in harm's way. I've had more lives than your average cat. I must be up to 20 by now.

Take these situations that happened when I was in a car:

• I was just maybe three years old when my mother left me and my older sister, Krystal, in the car as she went into the Highs Convenience Store. I apparently had messed with the gearshift. See, Mom always drove a five-speed, and would you believe I rolled us right into the front of the store?

• Then there was the time I caused us to go rolling down this major highway after I shoved the gears into neutral yet again. A taxi driver leaped out of his taxi, jumped in our car, and applied the emergency brake, probably saving our lives.

I guess I was too young to have those incidents shy me away from stick shifts. My first car was a five-speed, and I drove it off the lot without having ever been taught how to operate one. Seriously.

Hold on, u ain't read nothin' yet.

Me and my road dog Brie were spending the night together at her aunt's house in

Landover, Maryland. I think we were in high school, just kids really, so we were staying up all night long doing stuff. I was the girl from the suburbs hanging out with people who lived in the hood, so in some ways I wasn't entirely savvy about the dangers that lurked. Plus, the way they lived was different from me, and I didn't want to always eat and drink at their house. Many of them were roach-infested, and I was always terrified of roaches. Still to this day, if a roach moves in, I'm moving out.

So anyway, on this night I was really thirsty and wanted something to drink, but there was nothing in the fridge but water. At maybe three in the morning, I said, "Sabrina, walk to the store with me. I want to get a soda."

"Seriously?" she asked. "Now?"

"Yeah, come on."

"Girl, I don't feel like it."

"Okay, well, I'm going by myself then." I think she tried to talk me out of it, but if ever I wanted something bad enough, no one could change my mind.

You know, 7-Eleven is open 24 hours, so what the hell.

There I was heading out on my own, in the middle of the friggin' night, on Landover Road, Route 202. It was then that I heard someone coming up behind me. I was street smart enough to know that I needed to cross to the other side and keep an eye on them.

Now I was walking on the side of the highway next to the woods, but the guy who was following in the middle behind me crossed the street too, to stay on my tail. And then he caught up and started to walk closer behind me. At this point, I felt like something was *really* up, so I crossed the street *again* and headed back into the highway median.

Thankfully, 7-Eleven was in my sight. But I heard somebody running up on me, so I turned around. Of course, it was him. Here is something I'd failed to mention: I had a Louis Vuitton bag in my possession. These Vuittons were very popular back then with all of us young girls. It had the "LV" logo all over it, and it was expensive. I also had these EK glasses with snakeskin across the top—also not cheap.

These things were practically a neon sign blinking, "STEAL ME!"

This was SO not smart for a young teen to be holding at three in the fucking morning, on an otherwise deserted highway. I mean, picture it: Teenage girl, Vuitton bag, fancy glasses. I set myself up big time, made this an easy caper on so many levels. Plus, the bag is a clutch, so I had it in my hand.

Again, I turned around, and the motion of my turning swung my arm up and around.

This guy just tried to grab my purse and keep going. But when I turned, he missed it on the first pass.

"Hey!" I shouted, "what are you doing?"

"Bitch, give me your purse!" he demanded.

But there was no way in hell I was giving this asshole my fucking bag. I'd worked a lot of hours to pay for it. It was the most valuable thing I owned. No chance am I handing it over to him.

"Give me your purse!"

"No!"

"Gimme it!"

"NO!!"

The whole time, I wasn't even looking at his face, just down at his feet. And as my eyes went up from his feet to his body, I noticed a knife in his hand. From there, I went up to his face, which had a stocking cap over it.

Shit. This guy obviously meant business.

Oh well, I figured. It's only a bag.

"Here, take it," I said, throwing my purse behind him so he had to go back and get it.

Unfortunately, he went and got the bag and came right back.

Damn. I hadn't counted on that. I just thought he'd take it and leave. Now what?

The dude was motioning to me as he was standing at the edge of the median. "Come on over here. Come here." This nigga was trying to get me to go into the woods with him! Like *that* was going to happen.

This was when I completely freaked out. I ran into the middle of the street, because even though it's three in the morning, there were a couple of cars coming. I sprinted in front of them.

"Help! Help! Help!"

Two of the cars passed me by, but the third one stopped. A lady rolled down her window and asked, "What's wrong? Is everything okay?"

"No, everything is NOT okay," I assured her. "This guy just robbed me. Now he's trying to hurt me."

But as this was going on, the guy was just standing there calmly watching me talking to the woman, as if he were waiting for her to leave so he could resume whatever he planned to try to do to me.

The lady gave me a ride to the 7-Eleven, where I got to the pay phone. (This was the era before cellphones.) I was just about to call the police when some guys I knew pulled up and asked, "Angie, what's wrong?"

"This guy just robbed me. Took my purse."

"Aww man, that was YOU?! Get in the car, man. We're going to go find this nigga."

I hopped in and we drove all over, up and down, looking for the guy for hours. But we never found him. The only thing we managed to retrieve was a Diane comb that had been in my purse. But the good news was, you know, I didn't die. If the guy had dragged me into the woods, all bets would have been off. They'd have probably found me with my throat slashed or something. But I was still pissed about the purse.

Now, if he'd had a gun, he probably could have gotten me over to the woods. I'd have had to figure out a Plan B. But a knife wasn't nearly as effective a fear mechanism to get me to willingly accompany him off the highway. I just knew I wasn't gonna go out like that.

Then there was the time I got into a bad car accident. It was with Sabrina again, nearly always my partner in crime. This was a year or two after the highway incident, when there were a lot of young guys dealing drugs and making money. Many of them didn't have cars, but they could do something called Rent-A-Rock.

Now, this isn't to be confused with Rent-A-*Wreck*. Rent-A-Rock was renting a car from a crackhead. You would give some crack cocaine to a crackhead, and they would let you drive their vehicle for however long you wanted to have it.

We hooked up with these young guys in their Rent-A-Rock, a Nissan Maxima. They're like 14, 15 years old, really too young to be licensed and driving. But we were passengers in the backseat of the car, speeding down the highway in D.C., toward the Stadium Armory and going probably 90 miles an hour. When we hit that sharp turn right in front of the stadium, they lost control of the car. And we started to spin.

And spin.

And spin.

And skid.

And spin some more.

And skid some more.

I couldn't see anything. It was like being on a roller-coaster inside a car wash. Everything was just a blur. I was feeling gravity pulling us this way, that way, every which way. All of a sudden—BOOM!—we hit the side of a curb next to a pole. But God must have had his angels on my shoulder once again, because if we had struck that pole, it would have torn the car completely in half and us right along with it. Our bodies would have been splattered all over that pole.

Instead, we hit the curb. Thank you, God.

We couldn't call the police. That was the last thing we would do. We'd have all been arrested.

At first, Brie and me were pissed at these guys. We were like, "Fuck you!"

Brie asked me, "Who do you know around here?" I knew a dude named Dana from high school who came and picked me and Brie up and took us back home to safety.

Never did find out what happened to those guys for wrecking a crackhead's wheels. The way that drug had people *kirkin* out, the owner probably would have been okay with a hit as a replacement.

Another brush with death, averted.

And one more: I was having some problems with Wayne before we split. After that incident at the hotel, he never stopped cheating on me and was just outright disrespectful. I was telling my girl Nikki (another high school friend) about the situation.

See, Nikki had a way with these drug dealers, man. She must have had that *good good* (look that up in the Ebonics dictionary), because guys would give her anything she wanted, and she would be playing them all at the same time. She wasn't even the hoochie-momma type of girl. She dressed like a tomboy and acted like one, too.

I asked Nikki if she had any friends with money that I could hook up with, just to make Wayne jealous, and she told me about this guy named Mick. Mick was BIG TIME. He was also a *playa*. Well, I mean, all of them were, but I loved that he was straight up about it and didn't

have requirements of me. I told him what was going on, and he schooled me. He said, "Man, I know how to help you get that bamma to act right. Let him see that if he won't take care of you, another nigga will."

Mick's plan was, first, to take a stack of cash and leave it on the dresser. That would send a message. He also gave me one of his cars: "Wayne won't let you drive his car? Show him you've got someone who will. Take it and pull up on him in it."

Mick took me shopping. We went on trips. He did some of the coolest things, and it was such a turn on to me. He would whisk me away with no notice. We would be driving along the highway, and he would all of a sudden say, "We going to Atlantic City." I would mention not having clothes or needing to go to work, and he would say things like, "Man, fuck that job. I'll pay you for your time off. Don't worry about no clothes, I got you."

Mick would dress me how he wanted me to look. I'll never forget the time we were riding along the highway, and he looked at me and said, "I don't like those earrings. Take them off and throw them out the window."

Crazy, right—that I found that attractive?

Well, anyway, he also warned me that he knew the ways he would die. He said that it would either be getting shot in the head or dying from AIDS, because he refused to wear condoms. I knew at that moment that I had NO PLANS to ever sleep with him. He'd come and pick me up from work. Then he'd make his drug stops. We were never intimate. THANK GOD that it didn't matter to him.

Then one day, Wayne called and made nice. My plan had worked. We hadn't been talking, but now my heart was softened to him, and I no longer wanted to hang out with Mick.

When Mick called me that day to pick me up from work, I told him, "No, that's okay. I'm going to catch the subway." And wouldn't you know *that the very same day*, within two hours of the time he would have picked me up from work and then made his regular drug stops that I accompanied him to many times, Mick and his bodyguard were both shot in the head and killed. And I would have been in the car with them.

My guardian angel came through again.

18 ESTHER #2

Esther #2 was Esther Shaker, my spiritual mother and everything you could ever want in a mom. She was the wife of Pastor Peter and was always there by my side to guide me, until she wasn't.

Once Peter betrayed me, Esther had to follow suit. This was her husband, after all, so she was duty-bound to follow his lead. But it was horrible, because I was going through so much at that time. It's the moment when I needed her the most in my life, the darkest period, and she was somebody who could unfailingly make it better. She would always do or say the right thing. She was very, very nurturing. But it all dried up and disappeared when I really needed to have her by my side.

I mean, I get it. Esther had to align with her husband. But because of that, I wound up completely devastated, betrayed by two people at once.

Every now and then over the years, she's contacted me. And I saw her one time when I traveled to Maryland to see family. I was still resentful, but Kelsey—who also had a strong connection with Esther—wanted to catch up with Esther and Peter, so I swallowed my pride and went. I spoke with Esther for about an hour, never really addressing our break from each other. But the entire time I was there, Peter didn't say a thing to me. He kept his word about shutting me completely out of his life, at least to that point.

There was another time when I went to Maryland to see an art exhibit of one of Peter and Esther's sons. Esther was so happy to see all her children together, because she viewed us all as her kids.

This time, I did interact with Peter and we spoke, but he was just so cold I wish we hadn't had any contact at all. Even my kids were saying, "What's wrong with him? I've never seen him like that." There was just such a huge disconnect.

Mind you, this was a man whose reputation I had defended every time people questioned his business practices. When they were doubting his ethics or character or saying negative things, I always stuck up for him, just as I had my own father. He turned his back even though he also had indiscretions I had never judged.

They had five biological children that I loved like my blood siblings, and each of them had their own shortcomings over the years, but that never caused them to be disowned. I guess when Esther told me that it was exceptionally special to not be a biological child of hers, because it meant I was "chosen," she lied. She threw me away like trash. It was the first time that I would question my faith, but certainly not the last.

19 FINALLY, MR. RIGHT?

AFTER THE CRAZINESS OF WAYNE—WITH all the chaos, all the cheating—I was just looking for a nice guy. I found him in David. He was a good man, which was hard for me to actually embrace at the time, because I was so attracted to the bad boys. I had to literally talk myself into it: "Angie, this is what you've been asking for, dreaming about, praying for: a man who will treat you like a queen."

We met at the Classics nightclub in Suitland, Maryland, while I was with Roachell. This is also the place where I met Lily (more on her later). David was very persistent in hitting on me, and at the same time I was doing my best to ignore him. But he wouldn't leave me alone. I wasn't trying to be rude. He was just really relentless. I kind of yelled my phone number out to him, thinking that he'd get the picture that I was barely interested and wouldn't bother calling.

Wrong.

This David guy called me the very next day and left a nice message on my machine. I remember exactly where I was when I listened to it. I was with Hakim, going over plans to get back in the studio. When I heard the message, I remembered thinking, "Ah well, he sounds like *such* a good guy. Maybe I'll call him." So, I did. And what do you know, he *was* incredibly nice. We discussed this cabaret I'd planned to go to, and his cousin just happened to be the one who was putting it on. We also talked about his having a daughter that he was not sure he would ever see again.

I attended the cabaret with my girlfriends. David and I kind of hooked up there, and he would not leave my side. I was there with my girls, and he was on my heels the entire time. It was cute, but at the same time pretty annoying. That was kind of the start of us getting together.

Our first official date was going to the movies. I forget which movie we saw. Afterward, we went back to his place and I spent the night, but he never tried to touch me, never tried to kiss me, nothing. That impressed me. Given my history, that was something incredibly rare. I typically had guys all over me from the start.

I was captivated by that.

We were never really apart from that time on, but I also never stopped struggling internally with how I felt about him. From the start, I had to talk myself into being in love with him. It was like, "Angie, this is a good man, and you know he's good for you. Let him love you. Try to love him back."

Chemistry. You know when you have it. You also know when you don't. And David and I didn't, really. But I convinced myself it didn't matter. I did everything in my power to be in love with the *idea* of him.

I distinctly remember driving down the street in D.C., coming from a club and talking to Roachell. I said to her, "Man, this guy, I want to like him, but he's just too nice."

"Angie," Roachell responded, "you know what we always talk about? How you want a guy to treat you like a queen? And this guy is giving you all the things you've asked for. He's calling you all the time. He's answering you right away when you call him. This man has given you all his time and attention. How idiotic of you to not want to be with him. What's your problem?"

Presented to me that way, it was like having to eat my asparagus. It was good for me. And David made me feel secure. I'm a jealous, territorial type of person, but I didn't feel that way with him. I was spending every night at his house, and he had girls calling him, he would talk to them on the phone, and I didn't care. He wasn't my husband. I wasn't his wife. We didn't have the titles of girlfriend and boyfriend. And I was cool with that. So, nothing bothered me.

Maybe that right there should have been a red flag. When I really care about a guy, I get suspicious, possessive. I was totally the opposite with David. I understood he had a life before me, and these women calling weren't dating him. It's pretty clear I was okay with it because I wasn't head over heels for him.

Another kind of weird thing was that he had all these Penthouse magazine photos up. Naked women all over the walls of his apartment. Every time you opened a door, there was another one. Didn't bother me. Even bigger than that, the girl he was with before me—and who he already had a daughter with—called one night and told him she was nine months pregnant and that it was his baby. She was due to deliver any day.

I remember the look on David's face. His whole countenance just dropped, and I was like, "What's wrong? Wait—she's pregnant, right?"

"Yeah."

"Well, you know what? I don't care," I said, not quite believing the words had just come out of my mouth. "If she's pregnant and it's your baby, then I'm fine with that. It's your child. I'm going to love it. It's no big deal."

Mind you, David already had a one-year-old with this woman at the time. Obviously not a lot of birth control going on there.

The woman had the baby, and we got a call from the sister of the mother who told us, "No way is this David's baby. It looks nothing like him." It was apparent she was cheating on him because this was someone else's kid. Dodged that bullet.

But I was still feeling sketchy about this relationship. In hindsight, it was my gut telling my brain that this shouldn't be happening. Too bad my head didn't listen. I would just beat myself up over and over and over.

I eventually started to accept that David was what I needed and that I should marry him. Our relationship moved very quickly. We got married in 1996, six months after we met. It was a pretty small thing, with only a justice of the peace and a few friends, but we still dressed up. I had on the wedding gown and all that.

Our plan was to do a big celebration for our five-year anniversary, which we did. We spent tons of money on it. It was like a renewal of vows. I convinced myself that I loved him the day we got married. I convinced myself that I loved him five years in. I convinced myself of a lot of things. But no matter what I did, I could never fall IN love with him.

The whole time I was with him, I planned all these vacations, romantic getaways, all this stuff to bring us closer together. I got the sexy lingerie and outfits, wigs, all sorts of freaky stuff to drive our passion. All of this while David continued to worship the ground I walked on.

But it was always tough. We were married for 16 years altogether, and 14 of that was unhappy. The thing that kept us together was probably our kids and our foundation in the church, though initially David was a practicing Muslim, while I was a nondenominational Christian. He would do the whole thing, including putting down the prayer rug several times a day. Initially, religion created a lot of turmoil between us.

What I didn't know before we married was that he had a big, violent jealous streak. David was very possessive, very controlling. I know a lot of it came from him watching his mother cheat on his stepfather repeatedly, and also his understanding that he never felt like he was good enough for me, that he never got girls like me and always thought he was more invested in the marriage than I was.

David lived in constant fear that I was going to leave him or cheat on him, because he never felt that he should have ended up with someone like me. He could never just relax.

I could be watching television and see The Rock on there and comment, "Oh, man, he's sexy," and he'd immediately cop an attitude. He'd be really bothered by that and say it was disrespectful to him and stuff like that. We would have these fights. He would never put his hands on me, but he still did some really violent things.

I remember one time when David punched out the windshield of the car while I was driving. He smacked it over and over in frustration, and of course his knuckles were all bloody. I think the reason for that outburst was that someone called me on my phone whom he was jealous of, and because I was really nonchalant about it, he grew even more enraged.

David also used to carry a tomahawk, this mini-ax that he'd have at his side. There was the time when he got mad while my sister Talia was staying with us temporarily, and he just started chopping up the speakers of our stereo. She was lying on the floor as this was happening and got totally freaked out. She scrambled out in horror, unsure if this guy was going to use the ax on her next.

I started to have the violent, bloody, gory, disturbing dreams I described earlier. I was seeing family members being bludgeoned and dying. Going to sleep became like going to war. And then my eldest son, Franklin, started having episodes where he was afraid to be in his room by himself. He'd be screaming in terror, and this was in broad daylight. Clearly, the negative energy in the house was impacting him terribly, too.

One night toward the end of our first year together, I just up and told David, "I'm done. The violence and bullshit is too much. I want out."

As soon as I said it, he went to the kitchen, opened the cupboard, took out one of the little ceramic bowls we eat cereal out of, and started breaking it over his head like a crazy man.

"Fuck it!" he announced. "If I can't have you, then I just want to die."

David was whacking and whacking this bowl on his head repeatedly. He busted it on his skull until his head burst open, gushing blood and some tissue from the top of his head.

"David!" I screamed in horror. "What are you doing? Stop it! STOP IT!!"

At that point, he calmly walked back to our bedroom and laid down on the bed, his head seeping blood all over. He looked like Jesus on the cross. It was so scary. I called the ambulance.

"Not going!" David said defiantly.

He refused to go to the hospital. The laws have changed, but back then they couldn't make him go. The EMTs were advising it, but couldn't force him. We eventually convinced him to go because he obviously needed stitches.

So, that happened. Lovely.

This happened too: I found David carving my name into his chest with a razor blade. Which I guess is a twisted way to honor me, but also showed just how much turmoil we were in, and he was in. He was drinking a lot at that point. He was a heavy drinker throughout much of our relationship. That didn't help things.

I started to cling more to my church, getting David to reluctantly attend a few times. It was weird, though. He vowed to go but assured me he would do the opposite of anything they asked him to do. If they said "Stand up," he would sit. If they said "Bow your head and pray," he would keep his head up and eyes open.

In addition to this, David's young daughter, who predated our marriage, came to live with us for a year. And this girl's mother tried to control our household from the outside. When she came from California to pick up their kid, she called our house and started saying all kinds of crazy things to me, totally disrespectful. She was writing checks she would later be asked to cash, if you catch my drift.

I threw on my Timberlands, hopped in my car, and headed to David's grandmother's house, where she was staying. I was enraged. I knocked, she opened the door and commenced to open her mouth, and I popped her in it. I commenced to whup her ass.

Let's just say we never had problems out of her after that.

I continued to try to make this marriage work, so we moved to Silver Spring, Maryland, and rented a home on Musicmaster Drive. How ironic, right? I would soon become pregnant with our first child. It was my hope that having his son would make things better, but it really had the opposite effect.

My reaction was to start to check out of the relationship. I'd begun to wild out. I had two kids now, and I was going out all the time, hanging at the clubs and entertaining my first love, Raoul.

David threatened me, "I'm snitching to the pastor." He told him I was running around, doing this, doing that. I was like, "You know what? I don't care. I've already talked to my girlfriends. I'm looking forward to having some roommates. Go ahead and move out."

"We're not getting divorced!" he declared. "I did not get married to get divorced. No no no no no! We're going to make this work!"

It was about this same time that I convinced David to start going back to church with me and to develop more of a friendship with my spiritual father, Peter. He agreed, I guess because he was trying so hard to keep me.

At the same time, we had a lot of little spiritual disturbances that were going on. One of those was the fact David confirmed that he was having visitations from some type of spiritual being that was telling him to kill me.

Yes. Kill me.

As spirits go, these were not my favorite.

David said it was an entity that he would see sitting at the foot of our bed playing a banjo. And while I was sleeping, this entity was purportedly saying, "Look at her. You hate her, don't you? You just want to kill her, don't you? You should kill her. Kill her!"

David tells me this threatening stuff, right? He also carries around that tomahawk, something he could easily use to try to kill me. Oh, and he also slept with knives under his pillow, which became a habit when he was young because he was always afraid of his stepfather. I forgot to mention that part. So many things could go wrong here that might end with me being badly injured or dead. Not my preferred way to be in a marriage.

I mean, let's face it: This was insanity.

One day I said to David, "What exactly do you want me to do with this information? Do you want me to have a conversation with your entity myself?"

"Nothing. Don't worry. I wouldn't hurt you."

Right. *That* was reassuring. I started reading deliverance books like, "Pigs in the Parlor" and books by deliverance minister Win Worley, to see how I might exorcise these demons. My son Franklin was also seeing things he could not explain. He would describe these visitations as things that looked like an octopus.

Now in spite of all of this craziness, David was still a very sweet, generally mellow guy, believe it or not. It was only after I got out of the marriage that I came to see the character flaws that had been there all along. I guess I was blinded by the fact he was so much the opposite of what I had experienced with men before.

For instance, I'd put money on the fact he never cheated on me. But he turned out not to be the person I thought he was. I came to find out he lied about little things. He was also—and this is big—accused by my sisters Krystal and Talia with sexually abusing Franklin. In addition to that, his paternal grandmother used to run a daycare out of her house, and there was a child who charged David with touching him inappropriately when he went to the bathroom.

I found out later in our marriage that David had pleaded guilty to this last sexual abuse allegation, for no other reason than to keep from going to jail, according to him. This conviction remains on his record, which made it hard for him to find jobs outside of the hardwood flooring world.

There are a lot of creepy things about this man that I learned after we parted that made it clear he was different than the image he presented to the world. It could have all stemmed from the abuse he received from his stepfather that forced him to sleep with those knives. That would surely explain the anger.

My sister Krystal thinks the man just lives in a parallel universe. All of these occurrences would later lead to my decision to request that David go through a deliverance—or as you might call it, an exorcism.

I was worried about the entity that was telling him to kill me, right? Even though over the years we had some great times and David ended up eventually converting to Christianity, this evil spirit had started to show itself. David would suddenly speak in a different voice and complain of demonic visitations. So, I got my spiritual father, Pastor Peter, involved in a demonic reckoning.

"David is a man of God!" Peter yelled at the demon.

"No, he's not, he's not a man of God!" the demon answered back through David. "He's a liar! He's a cheat!"

The demon definitely spoke in a different voice than David's. I heard it in him, and I've heard it in other people. He clearly was battling something evil that had taken up residence inside of him. It was also impacting Franklin, who I came to believe was also battling demons.

Franklin was five when David and I had our first child, David Jr., or DJ; then we had Kelsey 16 months after DJ, and Raven (our Disney World baby) four years after that. Kelsey was kind of our renewal baby, the product of us finally getting this marriage thing right (at least temporarily).

In the end, however, children were not going to save this marriage.

20 SLEEPING WITH THE ENEMY

AS DIFFICULT A TIME AS I was having with David, once I got pregnant with our daughter, Kelsey, I pledged that I wasn't going to leave him. In surrendering unto the Lord, the God that I served, I felt comfortable with the decision. This was three years into our marriage, in 1999.

There were, however, so many times that I was ready to check out of the marriage. There should also have been times when he was ready to leave *me*, but no matter what, he kept holding on to the fantasy of me, even when he knew I wasn't in love with him.

When I was five months pregnant with DJ, I went to this cabaret to work the door, taking tickets. There were plenty of girls who would party pregnant, but that just didn't sit well with me. This was a way I could still be in the atmosphere but not be looked at as a triflin' mother. David's cousin was putting on the event, and I thought it would be a fun thing to do.

Then Raoul came through the door.

Now Raoul, who I've already mentioned and will discuss in greater detail in the next chapter, was a guy who I'd on-and-off had crazy chemistry with. And there he was at this event. I was shocked to see him. He was shocked to see me, because in actuality we had just seen each other intimately.

"Hey, youngin'," Raoul said, greeting me.

"Hey," I said in return.

My face lit up. I could feel it.

David observed this back-and-forth, the way we looked at each other.

"Who was *that*?" he asked with suspicion.

"Oh, that's Raoul," I said dismissively. "He was my first love." I'd told David about him before, but that didn't stop my husband from picking up on the special vibe Raoul and I clearly had. I guess it wasn't so easy to hide.

When we got home that night, David couldn't let the moment drop.

"You know," he said, "I watched you when that Raoul guy walked in the door, and the way you looked at him. You love him. You've never looked at me like that."

"But look who I chose. Who am I with? I'm even carrying your baby."

I guess this didn't come across as terribly reassuring. It was hard for both of us, because it WAS that obvious. I tried so hard. I prayed. I talked to God.

"God, why can't I love this man the way I need to?"

Here is the thing that I will never disparage about David: his parenting skills. He was a great dad. I mean, he was a slacker after we divorced but terrific while we were together. Once we split up, he put very little effort into seeing our kids and didn't pay a cent in child support, at least not willingly. The court wound up taking $200 a month from his paycheck, and then he quit his job and that stopped.

David was a pretty good provider for a long time, though. He worked tirelessly. After Kelsey was born, we started a hardwood flooring company together, and he was quite a craftsman when it came to floors. He installed them. He sanded them. He finished them. He was great at it. Prior to starting that business, I was working at Giant supermarket and part time as an Avon representative.

I was doing really well. In fact, I was doing so well that Avon wanted to hire me as a district manager. I had spoken with Pastor Peter about it, since I had concerns about how this would affect my marriage. I have always been a go-getter, and anything that I put my all into would flourish. I'm driven almost to a fault.

See, David had dreams of starting his own company, and I knew that if I took on this position that David might become more jealous and resentful. But the truth is, I was trying to make my marriage work. Without me having to express my concerns, Peter said the exact same thing I was thinking. It's sad when I reflect back on it now, that I was actually being held back from excelling in life because I was a woman who should dim her light so her husband could shine.

Over the years, though, we did have some really great times. We traveled. We built some beautiful relationships with people in our church. But then things really started to get weird.

I'll never forget this time we were headed to Disney World, which we traveled to every year for maybe five years straight. On our way, our plan was to stop to see David's Aunt GiGi, who had not seen him since he was a young boy. GiGi was the sister of David's stepfather, who had raised him from an infant.

That's a pretty crazy story in itself. See, David's mother became pregnant with him by David's biological father, Carl. David had never met his father in person. He only knew his stepfather, Greg. I later discovered that David's biological dad abandoned his mother while she was pregnant with David, to take up with an around-the-way girl named Hazel.

Meanwhile, Carl went off into the military and married Hazel. They stayed happily married for more than 40 years, until her death just about a year ago. David's mother, Clarise, would never get over this. I don't want to confuse, but I'm trying to put the pieces of the puzzle together for you myself as I go on with the story. So, let's learn together!

Anyway, with Carl having abandoned Clarise, she was left without someone to care for her and her child. She then took up with Greg, who would eventually marry her and become David's stepfather. David spoke of his mother's and stepfather's relationship as being very volatile and abusive. They would do drugs and fight constantly. David also spoke of abuse from his stepfather—and fear, as I mentioned earlier.

After Clarise and Greg's divorce, David was no longer in contact with his stepfather. Which brings us to the story of our visiting his Aunt GIGi in Georgia. We had arrived in the middle of the night, and when we got there, GIGi acted as if she had no idea that we would be showing up there, although she was very welcoming and excited to see David and meet his family.

The same reception did not hold true for his stepfather, who we would not make any contact with for almost 48 hours. He was very angry that we had shown up and disrupted his life with his new wife and child. It was a big ordeal, and GiGi was so fond of David that she was very angry with her brother and wanted to have his head.

We worked through that situation, though.

Fast forward to another visit on our way to Disney World. We stopped at his stepfather Greg's house, and things got very weird very quickly again. See, we had started to build a relationship with him, and everything seemed to be fine. But I had this really unsettling feeling that we weren't welcome there, as nothing was prepared for us and everything seemed just kind of doom and gloom.

Here we were yet again imposing on a family member who said they had no idea that we were coming to stay with them, although David had assured me that on both occasions, each party knew. I had no reason not to believe David over the strange people I had just met, but these occurrences started to happen more and more often.

David's stepfather had finally admitted that his wife didn't want us in their lives, and so as quickly as this man came back, he was right back out.

Then there was David's and Pastor Peter's relationship. They had become like father and son, but for some reason David started to distance himself from Peter. Peter kept telling me that David was alienating himself and not returning calls, but then David would deny it. Of course, I believed my husband. Why would he lie about something like that?

Nevertheless, it caused a strain on our relationship with Peter and his wife, Esther. So, at this point, we were now casting ourselves away from our church, just as I was starting to resurrect my singing career (this time as a gospel artist).

We had already sold our home a few years prior, because we just couldn't keep up with the payments when the housing market crashed, negatively impacting our flooring business. We had rented a few homes up until that time,

when we ultimately decided we were going to move to Dallas, Georgia, to be closer to Atlanta in hopes of my finding success there in the music industry.

We had to find a place to live first, however. While we waited, we moved in with Roachell and her family—until things got bizarre with David again. Something just wasn't adding up. Surely everyone couldn't be lying about the discrepancies surrounding the dialogue that David was having with people.

I awoke one morning to David having a shouting match with Roachell's husband, Eric, that eventually led to a fistfight in the front yard. It had something to do with rent money that we owed them. Now see, I had been communicating with David about money and whether or not he had talked with Eric about where we stood concerning bills and rent that needed to be paid by us while staying there. Eric felt brushed off and said that David communicated absolutely nothing to him, and so now here we were with no vehicle (our van had just been repossessed due to non-payment) and nowhere to live.

Do you sense a pattern of David failing to communicate and ultimately causing rifts with people?

I quickly researched some apartments, and we moved out. The new apartment that we moved into was going to be the death of me. I was already apprehensive about being in an apartment, due to my stated roach phobia. I interrogated the management of the apartment complex prior to our move about whether or not they had a bug issue. They assured me that they didn't. Famous last words.

Just days into living there, we were being overrun by a roach infestation. I couldn't take it. I was ill. I couldn't eat. I couldn't sleep. I lost weight. It was horrific, to say the least.

The only thing that kept me sane was my hot and heavy emotional love affair with Angel. It was truly a rollercoaster ride, because just when I felt like things between Angel and me were getting serious and I would be out of this mess of a marriage at any moment, out of nowhere David FINALLY agreed to counseling.

Unfortunately, that didn't go over so well. We had one session, and David got angry at what was being told to him. It was all downhill from there. I couldn't take it anymore, so we broke the lease and moved in with my girlfriend Wanda and her family. They were a breath of fresh air, with a beautiful home and wonderful children. We all were really close. Our time there was truly a blessing.

After that, we moved to Georgia. I had found us a beautiful home there. My emotional affair with Angel continued, and as it

did, I grew further and further estranged from David. Things finally started to come apart completely between us in 2011 and 2012, and we both knew the end was in sight.

I'll never forget our last Thanksgiving in Maryland. David was really melancholy. He looked at the family and just said, "I know this is going to be our last holiday together." And he was right.

The reason things lasted as long as they did was me: for years, I couldn't bring myself to just put my foot down and say, "It's over." I was breaking his heart just being with him but not being in love with him, while on the other hand, I feared I would break his heart by leaving.

If I hadn't gotten pregnant with my little one, Juan, I might never have had the nerve to do it.

For two years, I had been engaged in the aforementioned emotional affair with the man who would later become my life partner. Once I relocated to Texas, it became physical and shit got real. It turned into a genuine relationship when I got pregnant. I went back and forth on whether or not to terminate my pregnancy, because I was still married on paper at the time, though long since divorced in my heart and mind.

By this time, I was temporarily living with the gospel sensation Greg Gammond and flying back and forth to be with my family that was still living in Georgia. I knew I had to head back home and break the news to David that I wanted a divorce. I would sit him down and let him know we were done, without adding the part about my being pregnant. To my mind, it wasn't necessary to put him through that.

It was also a matter of self-preservation. David had done and said enough things in the past that it made me concerned for my safety in this situation. For instance, one of the things he'd said to me before was, "The only way you're going to leave me is in a body bag."

There aren't really two ways to take something like that. It's as ominous as it sounds. My family knew this and felt like the man was kind of a loose cannon. He was so jealous and controlling that if anything had ever happened to me, he was the first one they would suspect.

I mean, I took the "body bag" threat itself with a grain of salt, but still, I was concerned enough that I felt I shouldn't meet with him by myself. So, this had to be done in a public place. I picked the restaurant Ruby Tuesday, where I felt I could tell him I wanted a divorce without him getting violent. But the double-whammy of adding in the "pregnant with another man's child" part could send him over the edge.

One thing at a time.

"I want a divorce, David. It's time," I said to him.

"Okay," he replied stoically.

"But listen," I added, "let's not tell the kids until they're out of school. (They had another few weeks of school left at this point.) Let's not put that on them right now. Let them finish school, then we can deal with it as a family."

David agreed. But wouldn't you know, as soon as we were out of the restaurant and in our separate cars, he rushed right back to the house, grabbed our son David Jr., and immediately told him I was leaving him. Then of course, DJ went and told Kelsey. And they both told my youngest daughter, Raven.

So much for keeping it between us until school ended. It was really fucked up of David. But I guess I shouldn't have been surprised.

I knew in advance how they would all react. DJ was very nonchalant, totally unemotional, didn't really act like he cared. Kelsey was extremely upset and devastated, crying hysterically, as I knew she would be. With Raven, I knew she just wouldn't want either one of us to be hurt.

"The devil can have me," Raven announced, "but he can't have my family!" She was willing to give her soul to keep us together!

"Just kiss each other!" Kelsey pleaded. "Just kiss! Just once! Please? Come on! Just kiss, and you can still be together."

It was heartbreaking.

Who R U?

I was just so angry with David for spilling the beans of our plan to divorce and causing this scene to happen when it did. He wouldn't allow us to prepare them the right way. It was extremely selfish. He was still thinking he was going to win me back, I guess, but that was NOT happening. Ever. Especially not after he just dropped the bomb on the kids without my consent.

Yet I still had to sleep in the house. I wasn't worried he would try to hurt me, because he was still attempting to reconcile. He was going to win me back in his mind. What he was practicing was magical thinking, pretending, "Everything is fine. We're not going to get a divorce." So, at that moment, he was making nice.

If Angel weren't in the picture, and I hadn't been pregnant, it might have even worked.

The thing is, I was also down with morning sickness and just wanted to sleep.

"If I didn't know any better," David said, "I'd think you were pregnant." But he'd had the vasectomy, and that eliminated the possibility of pregnancy in his mind. Thank God.

The cherry atop the sundae came after we split. I had all sorts of great stuff saved in a storage space. David told me he was paying for it. My whole life was in there, including all my pictures, memories, everything.

"David, are you paying for the storage?" I'd ask. "Do you need me to pay for it?"

"Nope, got it covered," he always assured me. "I've got it covered." And he just stopped paying for it. He let it all go. It was just spiteful. But that's my ex-husband.

21 MY FIRST LOVE

THERE IS ALWAYS ONE GUY who you connect with on every level—especially sexually—but for whatever reason it doesn't work out for the long haul. For me, that guy was Raoul Woodward.

Raoul was my first love. Black guy. Not Hispanic like his name implies. We were with each other in high school, but were never *with* each other, if you know what I mean. His family loved me. I loved them. Raoul and I loved each other. But we could never come out with that love in high school because I wasn't cool enough to show around. That sounds totally superficial, but you know, that's what high school was all about.

I was that nice girl you could love secretly, but I didn't fit the mold of what was popular then for a young woman. I wasn't the girl you wanted to be seen with in public on your arm.

Therefore, he and I had a private relationship. We would do things together, but not where everyone else could see us.

That included a *very* sexual relationship.

But I accepted the rules that Raoul wanted to live under. That included our not going to my high school prom together. I went instead with my girlfriend Nikki and her boyfriend, then to Raoul's house right after.

He wasn't exactly a boyfriend. It was both a deeper relationship and a shallower one at the same time. I can look back now that I'm older and see that I was more of a sex partner for him, a glorified booty call. But what complicated things more was how we could stop seeing each other and then pick up again months or even years later and have it be just as loving and intense as before.

Plus, his family loved me so much that I could stroll into his house like I lived there. His mom in particular adored me. She didn't know the extent of what our relationship was or wasn't, but she thought I was the greatest, and Raoul's whole family accepted me as if I were The Girlfriend.

One night when I had a falling-out with David, it was Raoul's house that became my place of refuge. Things were very volatile with David and me. There was a battle between my Christianity and his Muslim faith. He was violent and it was a huge turn-off to me. I wanted to leave him, but he refused to let me go.

Raoul and I briefly became lovers again. On one night in particular that I went to see Raoul, I was pissy drunk and passed out. Everybody was looking for me that night when I didn't go home, and only my sister Talia knew where to find me.

I remember being asleep in Raoul's bed and hearing this banging on the door. Talia knew he was always my rebound guy. Now the sun was up, I was busted, and there was no way to explain this away except to tell the truth. Yet I lied, anyway.

"Here's what happened," I began my lie to everyone but my sisters. "I got drunk. We went to IHOP to eat, and I passed out in my car. I woke up in my car in the parking lot."

Who could possibly believe that bullshit? Well, David did, or at least pretended to. He kind of had to buy it because he couldn't face any other reality.

As we went through our lives, in my late teens and early twenties, Raoul could have a girlfriend, but if I called, she was made aware, "This is Angie. You don't disrespect her. I'll always love her."

One of the ironies of life was that as I got older, things changed for Raoul as far as I was concerned, because my looks evolved and I became the "IT" girl I had never been before. Of course, invariably, either one or both of us wouldn't be available. That's where the irony came in. He was in a relationship. I was in a relationship or married. Something had to be in place to stop us.

On the verge of divorcing David, one of my rendezvous with Raoul left me pregnant, and it was my brother Hakim who gave me the money for the abortion. I couldn't face Raoul. This would be the second time I'd gotten pregnant by him, and my second abortion. The first happened when I was right out of high school, at 17.

Yeah, Raoul and I never used protection. It wasn't very smart, since all you need to do is blow on me to get me pregnant. I happen to be very, very fertile, to my benefit and detriment.

I do regret those awful choices/decisions, and I have often wondered what my life would be like had I not made them.

But Raoul will always be special to me. We had a lot of great times and a lot of history together. And the chemistry we experienced is something you don't find very often in life.

22 WHO'S THAT GIRL?

EVEN THOUGH I ULTIMATELY STOPPED doing music to get married, raise a family, and give my life to the Lord, I always thought about it. It was reinforced when I became more and more immersed with my church. I got involved with the Praise Team and the Worship Team. I sang and I danced. We had a lot of great times together.

Through music and spirituality, I found at the Glory Cloud Church comfort and solace and strength and a sense of belonging, a sense of family. We were this small, family-style church that was really moving in the spirit of God. People would be praying in tongues. We'd be casting out devils. We'd be feeding the homeless. We were all just sold out for God and very authentic.

Nothing was about money. Nothing was about power. Nothing was about politics. We had so many young people as part of the church. These kids could have been out on the street, but instead they were ministering to people at their schools and in their communities and creating this movement of worshiping God.

It was so wonderful to be a part of it all. I was chosen to be the leader of the Praise Team. It wasn't a position I sought. It was Pastor David who insisted I do it. I didn't feel like I was the best qualified. I didn't feel like I was the best singer. We had some women on that team who could sing circles around me, but the pastor thought I had a leadership ability and a skill set that made it a good fit.

But then over time, it seemed like everything at the church changed. This would have been 2007, 2008. Power and money took center stage. Things got really political. Everyone started fighting, including the pastors. And I rubbed up against this opposition. The pastor's wife was jealous of me being Praise Team Leader. It grew so volatile and traumatic, and I started to feel controlled, with all kinds of pushback and negativity.

The pastor's wife wanted to head it up and be the one who was always singing—and she couldn't really sing. There's a big problem. It all left such a bad taste in my mouth that I stepped down from the position. I don't do well when people say, "You need to just be quiet and do what you're told."

My spirit was crushed. I was shaken with disappointment and bitterness and anger at what jealousy and power and money had destroyed. I just wanted out. Didn't want anything else to do with the church. This whole mess turned me off to spirituality, to music, to everything. The toxicity of it all destroyed my soul.

In 2008, I wrote a letter explaining why I was stepping down and leaving that church entirely. I wanted nothing to do with them or with music.

One day, my then-husband David could see I was in a bad place and asked me if I had a passion, something I would do for free if I could.

"Well," I replied, "I thought it was music."

With that, David started to build me a makeshift recording studio in the basement of our home, to try to reignite this in me, because I was so broken by what had happened at the church.

"Angie," he said to me, "you're supposed to sing. That's your passion. That's your gift. You need to do this."

"I believe that if I do it," I admitted to David, "I'm going to lose my family."

"And if you don't do it," he replied, "you'll resent me and I'll still lose you."

For that reason, and what I had endured at Glory Cloud Church, I would never go downstairs to that studio. David would be there and would be like, "When are you coming down here to start writing? When are you going to start up?" I'd just been so battered and abused and turned off by the church experience that it took me a while to get over it. Plus, I really did fear that once I went back, I'd be all in, and it *would* distance me from the family.

But I finally decided, "You know what? Okay." And I called up brother Hakim, who I'd been working with all those years before in New York. I wanted to get involved in the gospel industry, which at that time was just starting to really flourish. Hakim didn't have any direct link to gospel, but he had connections all around the business, so he was like, "Man, let's do this."

I started taking trips to New York to spend time in Hakim's studio and just be in that atmosphere. One thing I know is that I have an amazing songwriting ability. I could sit down right now and write a great song in five minutes. Writing with the melodies comes easily to me.

The songs started to flow. The connections began to happen. I began singing at churches and at little gospel clubs with open mic nights that centered on gospel and Christian music. Some gigs followed. I hooked up with some incredible background singers who, quite frankly, could sing me under the table. Yet I began to develop a following in the gospel world. I got more gigs. I won a contest to have my song "Wishing You Were Here" featured on the soundtrack for the movie *Saving God*, starring Ving Rhames. I was in my element!

The thing is, I'm not a true gospel artist. I can't blow pipes like a Shirley Caesar and holler and scream. I'm really an R&B singer. I'm more of a balladeer songstress, very subtle. White people have always loved my voice. For that to happen, you have to be much more conservative tonally, softer and more melodic. That's what the Christian music world favors.

In gospel—more so than my voice—it was the fact that I'm such a likeable person with a gift, an anointing, that helped me to break in. My promotion and marketing were very strong. It allowed me to share the stage with some major artists, like Yolanda Adams, Hezekiah Walker, Kirk Franklin, and others. I was even asked to perform in 2009 at the 24th Annual Stellar Gospel Music Awards, which was a big deal. That year, it showcased urban gospel music. That had never been done before. I'd made history.

I'd get put onto all of these things where people didn't know who I was. There were these whispers where people couldn't figure out why I was being highlighted. I was booked onto gospel cruises to sing. There were a lot of upcoming, independent artists who wanted to be in the position I was.

What I had over them was an ability to be in people's faces and have them never forget me. My brand—with the bright red hair—I'm sure helped me with that. I had an unforgettable presence, and still do. That's not boasting. It's fact.

Some big artist like Marvin Sapp and Yolanda Adams would be asking, "Who's that girl? She's everywhere we are."

To accompany this sudden notoriety In 2009, I released my first full album, a CD with gospel undertones called *Lessons in Love*. It helped me further build my brand. The concept for it came from my life story, and the "life music" was designed to carry the Lord's message.

My crowning achievement and my signature song on the album is called "Who R U?," and it resulted in an amazing video I'm incredibly proud of. The experience of writing it was like nothing I'd ever had before. It felt positively supernatural, like I wasn't the one holding the pen, as if it wrote itself. I was just the human conduit for a truly spiritual encounter.

Here are those lyrics:

Sitting at home all alone
Trying to figure out which way to go
'Cause my mind says yes, but my spirit's saying no
See deep inside I know what's best
But now I'm being put to the test
'Cause you see my flesh is weak
But greater is He in me

So tell me who, who r u?
To say I'll never change
That I'll always be the same
Now tell me who, who r u?
To say that I'm not saved
And that God didn't change my name
Tell me who, who r u?

To try and tell me my fate
That it'll always be this way
Who r u?

Now how can it be
That when I've given my testimony
That with me you'll praise
But behind my back all you do is judge me
And it hurts so deep inside
'Cause God says we're to love everybody
We've gotta be more like Christ
Then everything will be alright

So many times
We fuss and fight
Asking God why the people of the world
* can't feel the love of Christ*
It's because we say His name
But we don't change
Or represent God with the love that he's
* called us to proclaim . . .*

Mind you, musically I don't feel the song is necessarily that strong. It's a little offbeat. It's not necessarily powerful instrumentally. But it was by far the most impactful song out of the 16 tracks on the CD. Ironically, I recruited college students to do the "Who R U?" video. It cost me all of $1,000. And I mean, this video ran circles around any other video in either the gospel or secular music industries at the time.

In gospel, see, it was frowned upon to promote yourself and put all this money out there to try to become famous. It was thought to be unseemly. It was supposed to happen organically, I guess. But I was unapologetic. I felt good about what I was doing. I just aimed to do everything with excellence and see where it all led.

You just wouldn't believe what navigating the gospel business was like. At least you know who the sharks are in the secular world. In gospel, you don't discover it until you get behind a closed door and someone makes a pass at you, or you find out all the different artists who are sleeping with each other's wives and husbands. All they do is preach about not fornicating—and then fornicate like crazy.

Also, the year I did it, the Stellar Awards had moved to the Grand Ole Opry in Nashville. We were staying at one of the hotels, the Sheraton. I'll never forget how one of the employees disclosed to me, "During this weekend, we have the highest rate of pornographic pay-per-view movie use of any other time all year."

I guess I shouldn't have been shocked.

This whole time, I felt like I was making progress on building a music career. People knew who I was. I was everyone's favorite redhead. I got the live shows. I got the concerts. I got the TV shows. I even became a TV correspondent on the red carpet for events and hosted a television show. Many of my fellow artists loved me. I always got the interviews.

This career resurgence went on for about four years. But it was destined not to last.

The one thing I hated about the music business was how it would cause so many raw feelings among people, as with my friend Roachell. She did hair and dibbled and dabbled in makeup, but when the CD came out, I had professionals in my life like Kym Lee, who did makeup and was an artist to the stars—like your Whitney Houstons, your Patti LaBelles, and so many more. I worked exclusively with portrait artist Jackie Hicks. So, professionals like them had set the bar.

Because Roachell was such a close friend, I needed to give her a shot, even though I suspected she wasn't so great with the makeup. But I paid her to do it for one show. She could do hair. Makeup just wasn't her strength, as I learned the hard way.

I should have trusted my gut. By the end of the show, when I went and looked in the mirror, I resembled a freaking ghost. I was completely white and pasty. I was like, "Roachell's not ready, and I can't risk my reputation."

After this incident, I sat Roachell down and gently talked to her about it: "Would you be terribly disappointed if I used Germaine Williams?" (Germaine was another, much more talented makeup artist and was doing my makeup for the "Who R U?" video.)

"Well, I have to admit that I'm hurt," Roachell said, "but as long as I can be there with you when you do your shoot, I'm okay with it."

To make a long story short, with how my music career progressed and all of the celebrities I was around, Roachell grew upset that she couldn't always be with me, and that I didn't automatically call her if someone came into town. Her attitude was suddenly, "Oh, so now you're hanging out with your star friends and don't have time for *me*." She felt totally dissed.

The thing is, once you get into that circle, you've got to be careful how you move around in it and who you bring with you. You have to think of your career first. That caused me to lose someone who I thought was a friend, a best friend and godmother to my son DJ. She did some really shady shit after that, and I will not waste another moment discussing her. She is COMPLETELY out of my life. It's a tragic thing.

Anyway, the CD and my appearances backing it brought me back into the business in a BIG way. But I ultimately fell out of the industry due to a divorce from David and the manipulation and broken promises from Greg

Gammond. I guess I had been right. Getting back into music *did* break up my family.

Even though it was his idea that I get back into it, David knew my music would take me away from him. I started getting significant attention from other people. All of these voids were starting to get filled. I was being validated and made to feel important. I loved the limelight. It's where I thrive.

But after later moving to Texas to work with Greg, everything just completely fell apart. Even with Hakim managing me and the momentum we were building, I followed my heart and my new man to a new state. I thought for sure that I would have the best of both worlds, but damn was I wrong. This was the second time that I left Hakim hanging, and he said it too.

"Man, you left me," he told me. "We were doing big things, and you checked out. Again."

Yeah, that was probably true. But with the crap I got into with Greg, my divorce, and now being pregnant with my FIFTH child unexpectedly, I needed to be there to help my children heal. Hell, I needed to heal myself. This would become more important than anything.

What went down with Greg? There's no doubt the man killed my brand. The story ain't pretty, and neither is he.

Read on.

23 NIGHTMARE ON GREG STREET

I KNOW THIS PROBABLY WON'T come as a shock to anyone, but people are not always everything they appear to be. In fact, sometimes they are far from it.

Take Greg Gammond. He's a big star in the gospel music world. He's won all kinds of awards, including a Grammy. Highly respected guy. Has a great gift. Somebody I looked up to and was an idol of mine at one time. But he could be so much bigger than what he is if he gave to others instead of stifling their growth, their creativity. It turns out he's the world's biggest narcissist.

Little did I know when I moved in with the man that I would be living a nightmare with Freddy Krueger himself. Greg Gammond was a Dream Killer, as so many in the industry also discovered.

I connected with Greg on a One Love Gospel Cruise music event sponsored by the urban network Radio One, in 2010. I was an artist on their annual cruise for four straight years, the first time with fellow Neo Soul Gospel artist and friend Cynthia Jones, the second with my friend Roachell and a fellow independent artist named Tanya Dallas-Lewis.

It wasn't until the third cruise that I met the man who would later become the father of my fifth child, Mi Papi Chulo, Justino, a.k.a. "Angel Black," who served as Greg's bodyguard. We had a good time on that cruise, and Angel and I became fast friends. When he came to Baltimore with Greg for a concert, he invited me out with the lure of comp tickets.

The year after, on my fourth and final cruise, I'd brought my friend Lily. That's when we were promoting my title track song from the movie "Nocturnal Agony." Greg tried to push up on me when I started doing promo tours in Texas, but I was smitten with Angel (the forbidden fruit). Besides, when I told him I was married, Greg immediately backed off. Affair scandals aren't good for business when you're a gospel king. Not that it usually seemed to stop him from his many other indiscretions.

Lily is a cute, shapely girl, and Greg—who was by this time long divorced from his wife— noticed. He liked Lily immediately and stuck to us like glue. I hooked them up, and after the cruise, Greg was flying her in and out of his home in Cedar Hill, Texas, every weekend. They obviously hit it off pretty well.

Meanwhile, I got to know Greg because Angel was always getting me backstage passes to Greg's shows and seeing me there. I was living in Dallas, Georgia, at the time, so when Greg arranged for him and Lily to get liposuction surgery, it was in Atlanta with a famous surgeon near where I lived. That was when Greg offered to pay me to come and assist Lily during her surgery, because he was busy on a music video shoot with the singer Monica and the gospel artist James Fortune.

Let me just tell you something here about liposuction. It's a heck of a lot messier than you imagine. You're awake, just a little sedated, and they're poking holes in you and sucking fat out. The doctor invited me in to witness it and showed me the process, including how the skin is smoothed out while you go.

This is to say nothing of the aftercare, which is a doozy. You can't just get on a plane and go anywhere right away. You've got to lay in bed with either trash bags or sheets of plastic protecting what you're on, because you're leaking blood and fluid from all these little holes. It was gross! There is nothing neat and clean about liposuction. I guess I never thought about it. But of course, your bodily liquids start seeping out, because they'd stabbed you with a tube that's sucking fat from you.

But it's also more than that. This doctor wasn't just known for taking your weight off. He would also be sculpting and contouring your body at the same time, evening things out. So, there was an art to it. Unfortunately, you also needed to wrap yourself in all these little body girdle things to hold your shape.

I'll bet this is starting to sound like something you want to do, huh?

Taking care of Lily back at the hotel, the poor girl was stiff as a board.

"Oh, God!" she complained. "It hurts! This is crazy. Why did I do this? Why?"

"You want to look good for Greg, remember?" I reminded her.

"Oh yeah."

I spent a couple of days at that hotel holding Lily's hand, taking care of her, fussing over her. That's when Greg came by to offer me a job. We went out to grab a bite.

"Look," he said, "I really appreciate what you've done for Lily and me. I'm working on a lot of television, movie, and music projects going forward. You seem to have great energy and a solid work ethic. You really got down in the trenches with Lily, and that's the kind of thing I'm looking for on my team."

"Oh wow," I replied. "That sounds terrific. Let me just go back home and discuss it with my husband."

"I really want to help your career as an artist, Angie," Greg said. "I know it's your dream, and I think there's a lot I can do for you."

"Thank you. I'm in. This IS my dream. Just give me a few days to work things out with my family."

David and I talked about it. We had been wanting to move to Texas, anyway. The plan was, I would get everything set up and established, then bring the family.

That last part never happened.

A few days later, I hopped on the tour bus with the crew and was on my way to Texas. Lily was on that bus, too. She would now be Greg's live-in girlfriend, and I basically became the live-in personal assistant. That was not a part of MY plan. It was supposed to be about him helping me push forward in my career, but that's not how it turned out at all. I soon found out this was just Greg's MO, to use you for what he needed without bothering to help elevate you.

The motivational speaker Jim Rohn was known for pointing out that the more you help people get what they want, the more successful you become. Greg basically had the opposite view in keeping everybody down.

I did things that I never, ever signed up to do, like take his kid to school and bring him home. Pick up his dry cleaning. Shop for his groceries. Mind you, I wasn't supposed to be coming in as a personal assistant at all but someone he was going to groom to be part of his music empire. I was never told I'd be a glorified errand girl—actually, not even glorified.

He was also only paying me $500 a week, not nearly enough to send for my husband and children and have them there with me. Instead, I flew home every month for a weekend so I could be with the kids.

Seeing a man like Greg operate up-close was just devastating. To have to live with such a malignant narcissist soured me on the music business entirely. Dealing with him was just mind fuck after mind fuck after mind fuck. I thought I was going to completely lose myself. I almost did.

It even got bad for Lily. She slept with this guy. She would come downstairs and say, "Oh my God, Angie. Help me. This guy is crazy." She was obviously in it for the money and the perks, but she had to endure a lot of torture for what she got out of the deal. She went on tour with him, traveled, met all these big celebrities, drove fancy cars. But she paid for it in other ways.

"You are in for the ride of your life with this guy," Greg's executive assistant at the time told us on day one. "You've made a big mistake. Just be careful."

I'll give you an example of the insanity.

Because David and I owned a hardwood flooring company, Greg hired David to redo his floors. My husband drove from Georgia to install them for Greg at a really, really, really low price. Greg always nickel-and-dimed people. Never wanted to pay them what they were worth. But I still thought we should do the job, as it could lead to other jobs. Right?

We needed to collect a third of the deposit so David could buy the materials. Then we got the other third when we started and the last third of the deposit when we finished. But because the invoice was written for $333.33,

Greg was just livid. He gave me a tongue lashing for ripping him off. He trashed my name to some of the artists he was working with.

Finally, one of the guys on his latest project took Greg aside and told him, "Greg, $333.33 is a third. What are you talking about? No one is ripping you off."

"Oh," Greg said, surprised. But he would never apologize.

No, what Greg thought was that he was God, that he could do no wrong, and no one dared challenge him. There were big-time gospel artists like Kirk Franklin and Donnie McClurkin who would come over to the house to try to talk some sense into Greg, so they could work together. But he found it pretty much impossible to listen to reason.

There were just so many secrets and lies in that house. We found out from the very beginning, from people who worked in the house with him, just to be really careful about stuff. Even his own brother would warn us. That included his escapades with other women, how he was paying off people so they wouldn't share information about what went on between him and these women, how he screwed people over, how he worked people like slaves, how he made promises he never kept.

A man of God, right? How many men of God demand that you sign a nondisclosure agreement? (I never signed mine, which is why I'm able to speak freely here.)

Greg would also become a liposuction pin cushion after I started working for him. He had multiple procedures, everything from his stomach to his neck. I assisted Lily with him. He's a big guy, so just rolling him over required two of us. He was just this bloody, gory, fluid-y mess. Yeech. But I guess he felt he had to do it. The man loves to eat. This was his way of managing his weight.

I know this sounds catty, but my girl Lily had a much better body before she started in with the liposuction. What people don't realize is, when you suck out the fat that way, the body is so smart. It tries to get back what it lost too quickly. So, the fat starts returning, just not entirely to the areas where it was originally sucked from. You can wind up with a big patch of fat on your back or your shoulders. You're always having to keep getting surgery to even yourself out, and your body is always fighting to get back to where it was.

This, to me, is no way to live. I'd rather try to have a more restricted diet, try to exercise and eat a little bit better. Because I mean, Lily had a gorgeous shape before. When her weight started coming back, instead of having this nice hourglass shape of a behind, it became this exaggerated bubble butt. It's just not natural.

Did Greg ever help me with my artistry? No. Not once. I got a credit on one of his CDs just because I helped him with putting the project together, working with the artists, booking their flights, reading over and editing the songs, that type of stuff. But that was it. Nothing with my music career. If anything, being with him killed my brand instead of building it. I was very popular until I got involved with him.

Things finally came to a head with Greg in the most traumatic fashion imaginable.

Lily was still with Greg but had started creeping with one of the guys Greg was working with, Vic Holly, who at one time was part of a very popular R&B quartet, called Blackstreet. She was looking to go meet and hook up with Vic in Maryland. But she had two kids who lived there with her, Greg, and myself. One of them, Tanesha, was 16, a high school student.

Now, this daughter had to be driven and picked up every day, to and from a school outside the district, because the schools in Cedar Hill weren't so good. This was a responsibility they tried to put on me.

"Listen," I told them, "this is not my child. I already have four of those. I don't want to have to be her driver every day." I would do it to help out my friend if she needed it, but ultimately, I wasn't a babysitter. They needed to know that.

Anyway, Lily was off with her new guy this one night. I was out with Angel, and now three months pregnant with his child, though I hadn't told him or anyone else yet. I wasn't sure I was going to keep it. This was an extremely emotional time for me. I had a lot of things to consider. While we were out, Greg texted me and said something about needing me to take Tanesha to school the following morning.

I was really bothered by this because I hadn't intended on going home that night. I'm grown, and I wanted to stay out with Angel and talk things through. But finally, I just gave in.

"You know what?" I said to Angel, "I don't want the drama. I'm going to cover for my friend. She's in Maryland. Let me go and just do this thing."

I went back to the house and waited for Tanesha to tap on my door in the morning, indicating she was ready for her ride. She was a little bit late getting to me, but oh well. Not my fault. Took her to school.

On the way home, Greg texted me, "Tanesha was late." I was rightly offended by this. First of all, I'd brought my ass home to do this for him when it was not my responsibility. And now he was checking me like this was my fault she wasn't on time. She's 16, so if she taps on my door late, she gets to school late. Simple as that.

I was having this back-and-forth text thing with Greg. When I arrived home, Greg started talking to me through the intercom (the house is so big it required this), but the speaker next to my room had gone out. So, he couldn't hear me. I ran up the backstairs.

I was boiling mad by this point. I was doing all these things I shouldn't have had to, and he was laying into me. It felt like everything was starting to crash down.

I rushed upstairs into Greg's bedroom to address him and catch heat from him face-to-face, but he wasn't dressed. I startled him. He grabbed his clothes and put something on, and we started arguing back and forth. All the pent-up rage from a year of disrespect just started pouring out of me. I was screaming, hollering, talking shit. I no longer cared.

"Fuck you! Fuck you! Fuck you! Oh, and FUCK YOU!!!"

I was just going off the deep end. Greg called up his brother James, who lived nearby and is also his manager. Now that he had backup, Greg started coming at me, and he's a big guy, yelling and spitting in my face. He lunged at me and, filled with fear and anger, I clocked him right in the jaw.

As soon as I hit him, James Gammond grabbed me by the neck, slammed me on the desk, and started choking me until I couldn't breathe. He's military, he's smart, he knows how to do this stuff without leaving a mark. Neither of them knew I was pregnant, but they probably wouldn't have cared, either.

"Stop! Stop! Stop!" Greg commanded his brother, probably because he feared a lawsuit more than his hurting me. James stopped but kept me in a chokehold.

Anyway, I called the police, and while I had gone to my room to gather myself and wait for them, James, Greg, and Lily's 20-year-old son had apparently concocted a story for the cops that failed to describe what they had done to me. I got sent to jail on an assault charge and had to hire a lawyer, go to court, the whole nine. I couldn't believe that I was the one heading to jail and he wasn't.

Obviously, my time with Greg Gammond was over.

I wound up spending a night behind bars, which was just plain nasty. I don't like filth, and that's all there was in there. There were young and pregnant girls. (I was one of the pregnant ones myself.) A lot of Wal-Mart shoplifters. Most of them were in there for $2,000, $3,000 worth of traffic violations. You can sit out a week behind bars instead of paying the fines. This was all new to me.

There I was, rotting in jail, facing an assault charge, three months pregnant with a child I didn't know I was going to keep, a baby conceived in trauma and turmoil. The officers at the jail were very nice to me and they didn't understand why I was there. Obviously, money and status worked in Greg's favor. Big surprise.

I talked to my sisters every moment I was there. I must have run their phone bills up, but they didn't care. Krystal, Talia, and I, we are inseparable. They served bologna sandwiches and donuts. I wouldn't touch the stuff. The conditions were deplorable.

Angel bailed me out the next day. Things were already getting so bad at Greg's before this incident that I had applied for an apartment and had already been looking for a job. Angel was staying with his son at the time, so when I got out, he put me up in a hotel for a week.

Thank God my apartment was ready soon after that. I heard through the staff at Greg's house, along with Lily, that Greg was quaking in his boots, worried that Angel was gonna kill him. He always feared Angel. He never quite realized that Angel was a changed man. He was no longer THE KILLER.

Angel had been coaching me while living there with Greg on how to deal with him, what to say, what not to say, what to do, what not to do. Having been his personal protective officer, he understood all of his nuances and behaviors. He knew everything about him down to his dirty draws. Lily thought she had it under control herself, but that was an illusion.

I was livid with Lily. Here I was, being prosecuted for something that never would have happened if I hadn't had to cover for her trip to Maryland. I never told Greg about it, either. I kept my mouth shut because that's who I am. Plus, the fact that her son lied with them and didn't protect me? I'm positive they bribed his ass. He was a bum, had nothing going for himself, and Lily's daughter was a spoiled brat besides.

I had to pay a lot of money for an attorney, but Greg consented to drop the case if I agreed not to pursue charges against his brother for assault. I refused to sign anything saying I wouldn't, but the judge was instrumental in getting him to see that he really didn't want to ruin my life, that we honestly cared about each other at one point, and that we should just let bygones be bygones.

But meanwhile, I was a mess, struggling to figure out my next move. When I tell you that I was close to aborting my baby, I was also scared, confused, bitter, even suicidal. I mean I was *thisclose*. I know that Angel didn't want to have a baby at the time, and I was thinking, "How do I break this to my children and my husband?"

I had been wanting to be free from David for so long, but I feared what would happen. David was no tough guy, but he was a little bit off, as I made clear earlier. When someone tells you that the only way you are gonna leave them is in a body bag, you should generally believe them.

I had a conversation with God about the situation I was in weeks prior, and I heard a voice telling me, "This child will not die."

"God," I said out loud, "if this is you, you're going to have to intervene in some kind of way, because I can't trust that I'm not going to go out and do this. It's all just too much. I don't know if I'm going to be able to make that decision without some kind of Divine Intervention."

Well, He did just that. I would eventually be sitting in a jail cell unable to get that procedure done, which would put me past the legal time frame to have an abortion in the state of Texas.

Angel and I had previously made an appointment to go and have this abortion done. He was not aware of the last one that I made on my own. Neither of us wanted that anyway, and in Texas, they don't allow you to have abortions without first hearing the baby's heartbeat. They also don't permit them in that state legally past a certain term.

So, we went in, I had the sonogram, heard the heartbeat, and we both immediately got

Who R U?

emotional. Honestly, I had secretly prayed for this baby. I even remember the moment that he was conceived. I was so in love with Angel, and I wanted to leave David so badly. This would be my way out.

"Listen," Angel finally said to me during that visit, "I understand your position. Just have the baby and give him to me. Don't kill my baby. Have it and give it to me."

I shot back, "I can't give you my baby! I'm not going to have a child and then give it away for someone else to raise!"

Well, God made sure that we would have this baby, and Angel and I would have to figure out a way to be together so we could raise it together.

Here I am with Kirk Franklin, a gospel artist who crossed over to the mainstream and a wonderful man. At the 25th Annual Stellar Awards in 2010.

With Jamie Foster Brown, the founder of Sister 2 Sister magazine, which was very big in the R&B world. At her home in New York City in 2010.

Me with Ralph Tresvant, the lead singer of the R&B group New Edition. At a concert in 2010.

With Erica Campbell of the gospel group Mary Mary, in 2010 at the Merge Summit in Los Angeles.

Me and Tia Mowry-Hardrict of the sitcom Sister, Sister, at the Merge Summit in L.A. in 2010.

At the Merge Summit in 2010 with the great film, TV, and music producer Suzanne de Passe, who discovered and nurtured the Jackson Five. Vanessa Williams portrayed her in the 1992 TV miniseries, The Jacksons: An American Dream.

Who R U?

Here I am in Texas posing at the swimming pool at the apartment building of my favorite cousin Venita Benitez (we call her Sissy) in 2010.

Me and the great gospel singer Pastor Shirley Caesar during the One Love Gospel Cruise in 2010.

With the gospel artist Hezekiah Walker, during the One Love Gospel Cruise in 2010.

On the One Love Gospel Cruise in 2010, with the gospel artist Marvin Sapp.

Who R U?

With members of the gospel greats, the Clark Sisters, on the One Love Gospel Cruise in 2010. Left to right: Dorinda Clark-Cole, me, Jacky Clark-Chisholm, and Karen Clark-Sheard.

2010/04/15 03:37

On the photo and video shoot for my song "Who R U?" in 2011.

@LASHAWSPHOTOGRAPHY

At Left: Singing in the shoot for the "Who R U?" video in 2011.

At Right: I look like I'm back in high school in those pigtails, but it's the same day as the "Who R U?" lo-cation video shoot in 2011. I'm just trying to keep my curls between takes. Braided hair keeps the shape.

Who R U?

This was taken on the same day as the shoot for "Who R U?". I'm with my dad, Reds, in 2011, on Kennedy Street NW, in Washington, D.C. Don't we look alike?

Snapped during a family photo shoot in 2011. (Credit: Jackie Hicks/Fond Memories Photography)

This was taken during a 2011 GSRD Human Trafficking Awareness event to promote the fight against sex trafficking. That's obviously me on the far left, my cousin Sissy in the middle, and Mayor Maher Maso of Frisco, Texas, speaking at the right.

Who R U?

Working as a red carpet correspondent interviewing gospel star Kirk Franklin, center, along with cohost Chederick Cohens at the 42nd Annual GMA Dove Awards in Atlanta in 2011.

With Pastor Jeff Akers of Inner City Gospel, co-hosting a Dove Awards event in Nashville for Atlanta's "The C-Room" in 2011.

Who R U?

Hugging gospel artist Donnie McClurkin, on the One Love Gospel Cruise in 2011. He's just an incredibly sweet guy and I love him.

With Cindy Tawiah, owner of the hair-care line Diva by Cindy. I was the face of her brand for a while. This was at a 2011 event called The Diva Project, for which we hosted a day of healing, restoration, and transformation for women who were victims of domestic violence.

At the premiere for the horrible 2011 film Nocturnal Agony, *in which I had a song on the soundtrack. Good photo, though.*

Who R U?

Left: From a photo shoot for my song "Who R U?". Because black girls DO indeed rock. (Credit: Jackie Hicks/Fond Memories Photography)

Right: Me with my beloved Uncle Kirk Lawson, in Baltimore, MD, in 2016.

That's me on the left, MJ Precopio in the middle, and Molly Young on the end at my first Pure Romance World Conference in Orlando in 2016. I had an issue that nearly caused me to leave the event. These two made me stay. I owe my career to them.

With Dana Barish, my Pure Romance sponsor.

Taken at the Pure Romance World Conference in 2018, in Cincinnati. I guess I was kinda happy.

Now this requires a bit of an explanation. The dress I'm wearing at the Pure Romance World Conference in Las Vegas in 2019 is pretty hot, right? Well, I have five kids, and I breastfed four of them. I have no implants. How do you make your breasts look perky in a gown like this? Well, I went to Walgreens, bought some duct tape, and taped them up to give them a LIFT! My girl Mel helped me make the magic happen.

Who R U?

Here I am with Pure Romance President and CEO Chris Cicchinelli— a great man and a fantastic leader to whom I owe so much—at our World Conference in Vegas in 2019.

Blowing our signature kiss with my great Pure Romance team, the Zealous Zebras, in 2019. I'm in the very front, second from the right.

Who R U?

24 ANGEL OF MINE

ANGEL IS AN AMAZING MAN who helped to get me through probably the darkest period of my life. My marriage had been on the rocks, like forever. I was broken. Here I had been this loveable person on the one hand, then I made this one (admittedly significant) error, and now it felt like I was Jezebel. Like everybody hated me. It was just a horrific time.

And Angel (real name: Justino, pronounced "Who-Stee-No") was there.

A black Puerto Rican, he was with me through the dissolution of my marriage to David, through the difficulties with my kids, through giving birth again, through a *lot* of upheaval

That said, Angel also created more chaos with his behavior. He was a reformed gangsta and a longtime womanizer who, when we started living together, still wasn't in a place to settle down with just me. He had so many demons. He's still a little rough around the edges, but thank God he has come so far. Otherwise, this would have been another relationship to bite the dust.

But let's back up a bit, because the way he and I met was extra-special and fun.

There I was on the One Love Gospel Cruise, my third one in as many years. I had experience moving in these circles, so I was comfortable hanging out with the famous artists from that world. I knew how to connect with every type of person and personality. The way that I was with everyone was inviting, nothing offensive. My energy has always been intoxicating, and so everyone loved and accepted me. That's just my personality.

I was there with Roachell and Tanya Dallas-Lewis. I was still promoting my CD, *Lessons In Love*. Greg Gammond was just hanging out on the deck, so I walked up to him. We'd already met each other at the Stellar Awards, when my gospel music career was in its infancy.

I greeted him with, "Hey, Greg, what's going on?" He was just another artist on the ship, so I acted like we were all equals, even though some were obviously more equal than others, right? But he immediately hit me up for a favor.

"Can you get me an ice cream cone?" he asked.

Now, I could have easily told him to get it himself. I wasn't his assistant (yet). But it was THE Greg Gammond, and the ice cream machine was right there. Greg was a big man, he looked really comfortable where he was seated—sitting there like he was Julius Caesar—so I figured, "What the hell."

I brought Greg back his ice cream, and there was Angel, his personal protector, sitting beside him. Good-looking guy, in cool shades. We had an instant connection. I felt like he was sizing me up behind those sunglasses.

"Would you like one, too?" I asked Angel.

"No thank you," he said.

What I didn't know was that Angel was already well aware of who I was. He had seen me

doing a soundcheck the day before and was gazing down on me from atop the ship, thinking I was mighty fine.

Cut to later on. I had just left Pastor Shirley Caesar's cabin, where I had secured an opportunity for Roachell to do her lashes. I was walking to go have lunch when I saw Angel approaching. He stopped to say hi, and I saw this eyelash in his eye. Having just come from watching Roachell apply some false lashes just moments before, I guess it triggered my reticular activator.

I was about to stick my finger in his eye when I said, "Wait, wait, don't move."

"What?"

"You've got an eyelash in your eye."

"What?"

"Just be still."

I went in and picked this lash out of his eye, very carefully.

Angel looked at me, smiled, and asked, "Did you just monkey me?"

"Did I just *what* you?"

"Monkey me. That's how monkeys clean themselves. They groom each other."

"Well, then I guess I just monkeyed you."

"Now that we are already grooming each other," Angel asked, "would you like to have lunch together?"

"I would love it."

We had lunch, and it was wonderful. Coming off an elevator later that night, I ran into him again. He was coming back from grabbing Mr. Gammond some wings. You see, Angel too was caught up in this man's web of deceit and abusive business practices. During this encounter, Angel invited me to dinner in a private area of the ship. Man was this guy alluring—and that voice? Ever have a wet dream while you were awake? How could I say no? So, I didn't. But I was in a marriage. I couldn't pursue this, it was wrong, so I simply didn't show up.

This was in 2010, two years before David and I finally called it quits. But as we were disembarking the ship, I got off the elevator and, as fate would have it, there was Angel, again.

I think he mentioned something about my not showing up in that special place for dinner. I felt badly, so I thought I would make up for it by asking to keep in touch. I gave him my number, and as I was headed to the airport I got a really nice text from him.

"It was so nice to meet you," it said. "Have a safe flight back. You're the greatest."

The good news was that I was really enamored of this guy. The bad news was that I was still stuck in a loveless marriage. I made love to David the morning I got back while thinking of Angel. It was like this out-of-body experience.

It was very weird. Never had that happen before, or since. And David could feel it.

"Are you still in love with me?" he asked.

I didn't answer.

That's when my emotional affair with Angel officially began. We would text and talk often, and I quickly became addicted to everything about him. He awakened something in me that had been dead for a very long time, and people could see it.

One day, Roachell approached me and asked, "What kind of foundation are you wearing? Your skin is glowing."

"I'm not wearing any makeup," I replied.

"What? Oh my God, you're in love with that man."

I think I must have been.

People in church noticed it, too. They thought I was pregnant, I was glowing so much.

Things had gotten pretty hot and heavy between Angel and me. We began sexting, something I had never done before, not even with David. One night, I went out with some friends and came back pretty drunk. David would love to take advantage of me when I was like this. It was really the only time I could stomach having sex with him.

As he took advantage of my condition, I remember thinking of Angel and actually calling out his name. David abruptly stopped what he was doing and with a voice full of anger asked, "WHAT DID YOU JUST SAY!?"

I played up the fact that I was drunk and just mumbled some words. I don't know what happened next, but David interrogated me the next day. I treated it like he must have lost his mind and he left it alone.

It wasn't until we moved to Georgia that David found out about me and Angel. He had suspicions before, of course. I was reckless at times because the fire between Angel and I burned so hot. One day, David looked in my phone and checked out some of the texts. That's when it clicked for him.

"Are you cheating on me?" David charged, accusingly.

Of course, I just flipped it.

"What are you doing in my phone?" I fumed "You're violating my privacy."

I longed for Angel. I took any opportunity I could to fly to Texas for work where Angel resided. His messages were so mixed, though, and that drove me crazy—but it only made me want him more. PLAYA PLAYA is what I say about it now, but back then I was blinded by love, lust, and everything in-between.

Angel was all I thought about. He was my addiction.

I remember my first visit to Texas for a promo tour. I told Angel I wanted to hire him to be my personal protection for the time I was there. He picked me up from the airport in this old-school Buick. Any other time, I would have been embarrassed to ride in such a vehicle, but nothing mattered with Angel, other than just being next to him.

I could hear the song in my head from Prince and singer Apollonia:

I don't care where we go
I don't care what we do
I don't care pretty baby
Just take me with you

He took me to his home and we rode on his motorcycle. We ate peach cobbler together and shared the spoon. I just knew that I was going to let Angel have me. I longed for hot, steamy sex with this man that would not happen for three years down the line. Hell, I couldn't even get a kiss for two years into this situationship.

I mean, what the hell?! Was he gay or what? Why wouldn't he touch me or allow me to touch him? He constantly tried to get me to work things out with David, telling me that I didn't want the pain of a broken family. He also said that he had principles and that because I was married, he would not cross the line. This would happen repeatedly.

Although he wouldn't touch me, we would have some intense sexting sessions when I was hundreds of miles away. But then once I was in his presence, NOTHING. This was seduction at its finest. Endless foreplay, never a climax. Some principles.

I remember Angel's visit to Maryland for a New Year's show with Greg, and I met him back at his hotel room. I went there thinking this was finally going to be it! I was finally going to have him. We laid on the bed and talked for hours. I massaged his head and ran my fingers through his hair. I massaged his back—and still NOTHING! There was not one kiss, not a single touch from him.

This made me love him more and more, and he must have known it. It drove me insane!

Once Angel and I finally got together, it became its own rollercoaster ride. Again, he was a womanizer when we met. He didn't have that out of his system. This was unbeknownst to me, because we were in a distant relationship. Now that we came together, all the skeletons were rushing out of his closet.

When I moved to Texas to work for Greg Gammond, I was so excited to be closer to Angel. But would you believe, he STILL made no effort to see me for the entire first month I was there?

I would later find out the reason for that. He had not too long before resigned his position with Greg and moved in with a woman who was supposed to be just a friend. Well, she was just a friend alright. She too was in love with Angel and wanted to be with him, but he also kept her in the Friend Zone with the benefits of sexting and an occasional fuck here and there.

See, his car was not operable at the time, and he certainly couldn't have her bring him to see me. As soon as he got his car up and running, that's when our hot and heavy physical love affair took flight. Fulfillment in my sex life was dependent on an automobile!

We first made love in his car, in the parking lot at Joe Pool Lake. He "seemed" to be genuinely reluctant. He was concerned about our friendship changing once we became intimate. Well, of course it would change. But he had so much drama with women, baby mamas, admirers, fans, etc., that he didn't want to add another love-crazed woman to that list.

The man is a charmer, and once we were living together, he was still sexting with these other women. This went on for a few years. In my mind, it's an even bigger violation than sleeping with someone, because of the emotional connection you have while engaging in this. He still claims there wasn't anyone, but I don't believe that for one second. That may have been the case sometimes, but not all the time.

Angel should really write his own book. He's a reformed gangsta, which is probably where the original attraction came in. I love me some bad boys. He had an abusive, alcoholic father and was one of ten kids. He went to prison for murder many years before, and claims to have an identical story to that of the American Gangster in the film of the same name.

Angel still claims that murder charge was self-defense, but I'm sure that he was paying for many other horrific things he may have done while he was a part of that world. He still fights a lot of demons at 59. But he's also come such a long way.

Our son together, Juan, has really been like a savior for Angel. He actually delivered him, and the experience and the relationship has turned this man's life around. It's like he's getting to do things all over again, but the right way for the first time.

Nobody has ever been able to tame this lion throughout his entire life. Age has mellowed him, though, for sure. They say you can't teach an old dog new tricks, and a tiger never changes its stripes, but I endured his demons and loved him through them all. It wasn't easy, but that's what it took.

The Bible tells us that love covers a multitude of sins, and it's true. If you meet pain and bitterness and anger and strife with love, a lot of times you can break through things with people. That has seemingly been my calling throughout my entire life.

In terms of me having to sacrifice who I am as a woman to stand for Angel's bullshit, in the beginning I very much lost myself in the relationship. No one knew until recently. He almost broke me, but I quickly snapped back and finally *he* became more passive, attentive, and loving. He knows the gem that I am, and he almost lost me.

Actually, in many ways, he *did* lose me. He doesn't have the same Angie. I'm sure he would much rather have had the woman I was in the beginning, totally smitten and submissive to him. I have never been passive or a pushover, but early on when I was with him, he abused that, and I had to find *me* again.

Because I loved Angel so much, I didn't leave him during the multiple times I found him in sexting conversations. Normally, that would have been a deal-breaker, especially for repeated infractions. Definitely grounds for "Deuces, I'm out." Cheating is something I never endured with guys I was living with, only the less serious ones. If you have kids together, if you build a life together, you can't be doing that. When you're really in it with someone, the hurt is so much deeper.

There were times when I was lying in bed, pregnant with his child, when Angel was sexting with someone. Right next to me. He thought he could get away with it and it wouldn't be a big deal, because he was that guy nobody would ever challenge. No one could tell him what to do.

I mean, Angel had been the president of the Dallas Chapter of the Ruff Ryders Motorcycle Club. He was a bad ass with a huge ego. Those dudes did whatever they wanted. All the girls wanted them. So, he lived this lifestyle where he could treat women like that, and they'd put up with it because they wanted to be with him so badly.

But with the sexting, he would act like it was nothing.

"She's nobody, it's just my Ruff Ryder sister," he would insist.

But I was reading dialogue that clearly was flirting, that was absolutely inviting. That to me was crossing the line. In addition to that, there were a lot of emotional texts where it was clear Angel was invested beyond just friendship. It was engaging with women in inappropriate conversations that would lead them on.

I did NOT take this shit lightly. There would be screaming matches. Breaking phones. Crying. Throwing stuff across the room. I also knew what lines not to cross because of Angel's past. His mom was abused by his dad—I mean, abused like watched his mother get beaten

down to the floor, bruised up, bloody. I made sure never to get physical for that reason.

I knew that any actual violence would be a trigger for him, so I never put my hands on him and he never put his on me. Fortunately, other women are a non-issue now.

Angel never touches alcohol. His dad was a heavy drinker, so he never drank himself. He may smoke a little weed for medicinal purposes, a couple of hits just to relax and he's done. The man has led an active life, and his body is feeling the effects.

That's in addition to the bad things he did, for which Angel finally had to do time. He was a big-time drug dealer who the cops just couldn't seem to touch, even though he ran the streets. Couldn't bring him down. He was very smart and likeable, beloved in his community for taking care of the elderly. He paid a lot of people's bills for them. He'd buy all the ice cream from the ice cream truck and give it to the kids. Stuff like that.

Because people liked Angel, no one ratted him out. That made it hard for any charge to stick to him. Plus, he used to work in law enforcement and as a correctional officer, so he knew how to work both sides. He understood what to do and what not to do.

Then came the day when he was set up by a cop, at least according to him. He was in a club when a guy walked up to him and looked like he was going to start firing his gun. But as this event escalated outside, Angel pulled his gun and got the guy faster. Self-defense, right? Well, he still went to jail for it. It was a long story of betrayal at the end of the day, and he wound up serving six years in prison. This was maybe 30 years ago, so a long time in the past. It happened in Champaign, Illinois.

For a lot of years, as I mentioned, Angel was the head honcho. He was no nonsense. He didn't do any pimping. Didn't like for women to be disrespected (go figure). He was high up the food chain, so nobody gave him any shit. He was in charge.

I always say that Angel is the guy I'd always wanted to be with, all grown up. I like his tough side. I like to feel protected, and maybe that has a lot to do with not having been protected a lot of times in my life. This is a man who has had my back, and I've liked that feeling. What I don't like is infidelity, betrayal, mistrust. A lot of times, people will put up with it because they want to keep the lifestyle that comes with it. Not me.

I've tried to be that girl before, the one who sacrifices to be part of the in-crowd. But I've ultimately found I'm not built like that. I'm a romantic, a true lover at heart, and I can't be between two people. I can't be having sex with two men at once. I'm not capable of doing it. It's one or the other.

Poor David. Once my mind was made up to be with Angel, David was cut off from sex with me completely.

Now that life is all behind me. Instead, I can love and appreciate my man for the charisma he brings to the table, without worrying that he's stepping out on me. Both men and women are drawn to Angel. There are those who are jealous of him, too, because he carries that confidence.

But Angel still fosters regrets. He's estranged from most of his children (he has seven total). He has a crazy history where that's concerned, and I know that's something that he doesn't easily brush off. There was an ex who totally poisoned the kids against him, and *literally* tried to poison him as well. Fortunately, she didn't succeed.

There was a betrayal from Angel's mother when she sided with the mother of his eldest son against him, and it broke him. What happened was, Angel went into the military so he could take care of the child financially. He'd send money back home to his son's mother, who was living in the projects, and she wasn't using the money to take care of their son. She was blowing it on clothes and getting her hair done and wasn't being a responsible parent.

Angel came home from the service saying, "She's not taking care of him. I want my son." And that's where his mother sided with the irresponsible mother instead of him. I think she had probably just been taught that a child belongs with his mother no matter the circumstances, when clearly that's often wrong.

Angel didn't speak to his mother for nine years, and before that he'd worshiped the ground she walked on. Well, he still does. It just took him time to get over it. This is a woman who lived with a bullet in her face for most of her adult life. She had it tough. From the stories I've heard, she was a strong, kind, and gentle soul.

The bullet came from the gun of a man who didn't like the fact she chose to be with Angel's father instead of him. He tried to kill her, and so Angel's grandfather stepped in to protect his daughter and shot and killed the assailant. It was a very messy situation. Angel had a lot of trauma and grew up seeing a lot of death and abuse, and it's difficult to keep that inside and not have it turn into rage toward the outside world.

But you know what? I feel lucky now to have this guy in my life and to have witnessed his turnaround into the man he's become. It's a blessing that I never take for granted—and neither does Angel.

At the same time, I've established boundaries as well as expectations for what I will and will not allow, what I'll stand for and what I won't. That understanding breeds communication between us.

I look at relationships so much differently now than I used to, which must be an age thing. It's no longer about butterflies and giddiness. There's a maturity that runs through. Because I'm empowered and in tune with myself, I'm able to much more effectively keep my emotions in check.

Love to me is no longer a fairytale feeling but a function of sacrifice, of give-and-take, of mutual respect. In terms of Angel and me, it's about dealing with one another's baggage and helping each other through, about not running at the first sign (or any sign) of trouble. We have both been about healing and sticking around, and that's a wonderful thing.

25 MOTHERHOOD

I'VE MADE A CONSCIOUS CHOICE not to put too much about my children in this book. It is, after all, my autobiography, and they didn't ask to have their own lives held up to close scrutiny here. But since they are such an important part of my story, I also couldn't ignore them completely.

Franklin Robinson, age 27—He's been a problem child from the age of two. I don't know if that's the result of any abuse from the man who adopted him, the demons from my past that came about as a part of the lifestyle I led back then, or partly from having a biological dad who was a drug dealer, absent and now deceased. Franklin has led a life of turmoil. He blames me for his troubles, and I have no problem taking some of that blame.

But ultimately, his life and life decisions (good and bad) are his and his alone.

In my opinion, Franklin has had many privileges in life. Being the only child for his first five years found him getting all of the attention and everything he wanted as a small child (read: spoiled rotten). Raising him was very stressful, and there never seemed to be a moment of peace concerning him. There was always trouble, including calls from his school, day after day after day.

I did everything I could to raise him right. After a lot of time and difficulty, he graduated high school and eventually went to college. But ultimately, Franklin dropped out and did what many young teens do: slumming with friends and trying to become a rapper. Once he wore out his welcome with several people back home in Maryland, he came to visit me in Texas and was dishonest about being put on academic probation, and at the age of 25 suddenly had nowhere to go.

So, what's a mom to do? Why, help her child, of course. He was able to get a job, a car, and his own apartment, and then became (as they say) "woke." This new way of thinking caused him to become this person who didn't want to work for, as he said, "The White Man." Of course, I'm the bad mom because he felt entitled and somehow believed I was supposed to take care of him.

Anyway, I know he's not drugged out. But he's on his own journey. I offered to give him help, and he didn't want it. He wanted to do things his way, and so he is.

But I'm a stronger woman now and try not to allow him or anyone else to fill me with guilt about making the best choices for me and the home where I am still raising Franklin's siblings. He has been coming by lately to visit, and we are working on our relationship. He seems to be maturing quite a bit.

David ("DJ") Robinson, age 22—David was always really cool and mild-mannered. Never caused any problems. Very trustworthy. But he was also a little cowardly, because he would typically leave his sisters behind and run off if any drama went down. He never seemed to have much of an opinion about the way things happened, including my split from his father David Sr. He just brushed everything off, including my repentance for the way it all ended with his father.

DJ's time with me during his last two years of school were not always pleasant. He would butt heads with Angel sometimes, as my new man was not his father. There wasn't a lot of respect there, nor much tolerance from Angel. Ideally, I would have wanted him with his father, but when I found out that David was sleeping on someone's couch and had DJ staying with friends, I had to bring my son to Texas and take care of him until David could get his act together.

Both of them resented me for it, but I did what I felt was best and simply had to face the consequences. DJ has pretty much been with David or on his own since graduating high school, with honors.

Just when I thought things were getting better between us, he woke up and stopped calling me one day. That was two years ago. It hurt like hell, and I know that David has been instrumental in brainwashing him to X me out of his life. It happens far too often in families, and it's so unfair to the children to be put in the middle of grown-up bullshit. But that's often how it goes down.

During the editing process of my book, I have spoken with DJ and sent him money for his birthday, and he has messaged me on mine. From what I hear, he is traveling with his dad, doesn't have a job, and smokes a lot of weed. In other words, he still hasn't launched his life. But at this point, I'm powerless to change that. His journey is his journey.

Kelsey Robinson, age 20—She's like a little mini-me in business, working as a consultant for the same company I do (Pure Romance) as well as an aspiring (and published) photographer. Kelsey is a junior in college majoring in photojournalism and a would-be entrepreneur. She also tends to be somewhat meek and naïve. My eldest daughter leads with her heart, which is dangerous. I'm that way too, so I know.

But I have something that my daughter has yet to develop: street smarts. She is incredibly loving but easily manipulated. She is also broken by her father's shunning her and embracing DJ and Raven somewhat more, along with the repeated sex abuse that she has too often fallen prey to. I have tried to protect and support her when these things have happened, but

her father and her brother and best friend DJ, not so much. I know for a fact that it's caused her some deep trauma that she continues to battle today.

For this and other reasons, Kelsey looks for love in all the wrong places. Even at the tender age of 20, she needed to be saved by me from a pair of toxic relationships that were forming. She has never had an actual boyfriend and is a virtuous woman for sure, as well as trustworthy, dependable, and extremely nurturing.

Kelsey is in therapy, which I'm not completely sure is helping her; therefore, I try to keep her as close as possible. Her little brother, Juan, absolutely adores her and sees her as his second mom. Those two bonded from the start and have been inseparable ever since.

Raven Robinson, age 16—A junior in high school who has always been popular, Raven is a phenomenal dancer, loves music and acting, and is just all-around super-talented. She is also beautiful yet has a poor self-image and used to cut herself to release her emotional pain. I mention this as a warning sign to parents to be vigilant for when your children are hurting. This was all new to me.

She is more of a follower than a leader, which is shocking to me because she's someone people gravitate toward and would follow if she recognized that part of herself. In a lot of ways, the girl is my clone. She was very young when her father and I divorced, and probably for that reason it impacted her more than the other kids.

I'm sure Raven blames me for the divorce, and it's made us more distant than we once were. She has definitely been partially brainwashed by her dad and his current wife. She puts David on a pedestal. In her eyes, he can do no wrong.

One thing Raven didn't get from me is the amount she holds inside. She does not like to open up or express her feelings, and as a result she's consistently refused therapy. (Recently, she finally agreed.)

Raven craves the hood life as an escape from her safe suburban lifestyle. (Sound familiar?) She wants to be a rapper or actress but has no Plan B, no college aspirations. That was also just like me. You couldn't tell me anything. I had all the answers. Same with Raven.

Juan Pena, age 7—Little Juan is simply a joy. Super smart. Has a great heart and loves his dad so much. The boy is extremely intuitive. He has expressed his hurt over how his sister Raven treats him at times. He loves her so deeply and longs to feel the same love from her. Being stuck at home during the pandemic brought the two of them closer. That truly warms my heart."

But Juan clings to Kelsey who, as I mentioned before, is like a second mother to him. Their love and bond is so special. Though he's very mild-mannered, Juan is extremely gifted and talented. He's musically inclined and loves to dance and of course play video games (which he would do all day, every day, if we let him).

Juan wants to become a scientist so he can create more superheroes and is just an amazing kid overall. I'm often surprised at who he is, because of all the trauma and turmoil I was experiencing while pregnant with him. It obviously didn't transfer to him, thank God. He's all about love.

26 BACK DOWN MEMORY LANE

THE BRASS RAIL WAS A gay male strip club in D.C., back in 1994 when my son Franklin was a year old and his daddy, Wayne, was locked up. My girls asked me to go hang out at this club that I didn't even know existed.

It was like a modern-day Sodom and Gomorrah type of situation, like a Quentin Tarantino movie where you see demons walking around. It was essentially an out-of-body experience, yet so intoxicating—and so inviting and addictive to watch. I don't even think the term transgender was a thing yet then, but there were what used to be known as transvestites (primarily guys dressed up like girls).

You had purportedly straight guys who were there stripping for a male audience. The dancers would dance and feel on the guys in the crowd as straight men would a woman. And these dancers were all celebrities in that world. They could really dance. Their bodies were amazing. I loved the vibe and went back again and again.

While it was overwhelmingly men in this club, both onstage and in the crowd, every now and then they would have special female guests. I remember they featured one whose stripper name was Uzi, like the firearm. I recall watching her dance, and she was phenomenal. I suddenly found myself feeling turned on by the way she looked, the way she moved. There was this major attraction.

As I fought to resist these emotions, I said to myself, "Angie, you know why you're having these feelings? Your flesh is responding to the allure of the atmosphere, but you are a straight woman."

Meanwhile, the more I said this to myself, the more intensely I felt it. There was just no question, I was conflicted. The girls who brought me to the club were over it from the start. Didn't do anything for them. But I wanted to come back again and again. It was new for me, and I loved it. This other girl that my girls introduced me to, T.J., was also into it. She became my partner in going out to the Brass Rail week after week after week.

One night after leaving the Brass Rail, T.J. and I went home together. No words were spoken. We just wound up having a sexual encounter and repeated it a few more times.

Then I came home one night with one of the strippers, a man. His name was Loverboy. I was really starting to get into the excitement of the whole thing. I was just wild'n out! But I arrived back from the club one other night, and I heard the voice of the Lord say, "So, this is the life that you choose for yourself. But what about the life of your son?" Because remember, I had a one-year-old at the time.

This voice continued, "Don't you realize when you go out into these clubs and become entangled with all of these different people that you bring those spirits back to your child?"

I never went back to the club after that. I cut off all the people I had met and had contact with there.

It finally became clear, after my conversation with the Lord, that I was out there doing some crazy, wild stuff, and if I were endangering my child in any way, it just wasn't worth it. I mean, men and women were being raped and killed leaving the club with this one and that one. Diseases were running rampant, too. I was exposing myself to all of that. It was like it temporarily took over my mind and body.

But no more. I was done! When I look back over my life and take a stroll down memory lane, I'm sometimes shocked that I am still living and breathing. I was too often reckless. I must have thought I was invincible.

I mean, I was the wife, partner, girlfriend, etc. to so many different people who were heavily involved in crimes that it could have ended my life or put me in jail forever. The fact that I'm still here is mind blowing. I have lost so many friends, male and female, along the way who never got the chance to tell their story. It hurts my heart to think back on it, but I'm grateful for second, third, and fourth chances.

And I'm hugely thankful to have the opportunity to tell my cautionary tale in this book. Thank you, God.

27 FORGIVENESS

I TEND NOT TO HOLD grudges. Not even against my ex-husband David. I've always said that I'm the person you could get into a physical fight with, and then right afterward I'm fine, we're friends, everything's cool. We'll duke it out, and then I still love you.

I've tried to be that girl who holds things against people. But I love everyone too much. I care about people too much. I can't use and abuse people or think of them badly after we've had a quarrel. Life is just too short, you know? I think I just *feel* too much. Probably to a fault.

But I've gotten wiser as I've grown older, and less tolerant. I don't know if that's an age thing, because people say that when you get in your 40's and 50's, you both mellow out and at the same time grow less accepting of things that you might have let slide at one time.

I used to be the girl who really, really cared. It would paralyze me to lose a friendship. I just wanted everyone to like me. I didn't want to hurt anyone's feelings. (Cue the violins.)

However, I'm at that point in my life now where if you're in my space and you're negative and toxic, you can find your way with someone else. I can love you from afar, but I'm not going to be a doormat for anyone.

At the same time, forgiveness is essential to my peace of mind and growth as a human being. I do it for *me*, not for *you*. Holding onto poisonous feelings only takes me down. It doesn't improve anything or make any necessary point.

This is why I have to forgive you. It's also one of the most important lessons I hope my book drives home.

You can't allow people to change or define you. You can't permit situations and circumstances to make you grow bitter, angry, and unforgiving. I know some people who have lived their entire lives holding tightly to unhappiness, discontent, and condemnation—it's a dark and lonely path to travel.

When you're always blaming someone else for your situation, you stay stuck in neutral or—worse yet—reverse. You never have complete success. You rarely experience joyous relationships. When you allow unforgiveness to set in, you block your blessings. I've seen it happen time after time with people who have gone their whole lives just downtrodden, stumbling from one dead-end job to another, one abusive relationship to another.

These are the people who you always hear say, "They did this to me, and I'll never forgive them." The problem is that the only person who is really getting hurt in that exchange is the person who refuses to forgive.

But let's not confuse this. Practicing forgiveness isn't the same as taking abuse and staying in a bad situation. I just know that unforgiveness is the same as willingly drinking poison. It's a curse you put on yourself. Conversely, if you forgive someone, release them, and move on with your life, you've cleaned the slate and started fresh. It will set you free in a lot of ways.

The recipe for joy, for success, is not holding on to that negative energy. That's one thing people reading my story need to know. If they want their life to wind up anything near the level of success I'm having now, they've got to *give* and they have to *forgive*. *Give* and *forgive*.

Also, don't allow others to hold you captive to your mistakes. As you have read in this book, I have made many. If people choose not to forgive you when you've exercised accountability and responsibility, then that's their problem and not yours. You MUST forgive yourself and peace WILL follow. Once you have forgiven yourself, then you become a vessel fit to be used by God. Now you can pour that into others without poisoning them and watch the blessings flow.

The truth is, the more people you help to become successful, the more successful you will become yourself, so just give until you can't give anymore. Giving isn't necessarily supposed to always feel good, because sometimes you have to make a sacrifice. Giving your time and energy can be uncomfortable. It's time and energy you can't devote elsewhere. There is a huge blessing in that on both sides.

Give and *forgive*. Those are great principles to live by.

28 THIS IS ME

Our destination is predetermined. It's the journey we go on that's important.
C. S. Lewis

BACK IN 2000, I HAD an opportunity to sit for an interview for a Heritage profile that looked at who I was, where I'd been, and predicted who I would be in the future. It's an in-depth personality assessment tool that identifies your core motivations. I was already in my late 20's but found myself at a crossroads. It's interesting now to look back and see just how perfectly this book assessed me. Here is one of the early pages:

I AM ENCOURAGED WHEN . . .
* I am in the limelight.
* I am the best at what I do.

* I am thorough, organized, efficient, and effective.
* I feel connection, support, and a sense of belonging.
* I engage in brainstorming and the creative process.
* I am seen, acknowledged, and validated for who I am.
* I express excitement, energy, and enthusiasm.
* I acknowledge and celebrate closure in projects.
* I take the ball and run with it.
* I balance speed with excellence.
* I keep a positive, optimistic perspective.
* I have freedom, flexibility, and variety.

It's kind of amazing just how dead on this was. I mean, basically, the bottom line was that I needed to be in control and allow my creativity to flow. But the way this profile was constructed established it in a particularly vivid fashion.

Here are some of the other appraisals:

I'm a Free Spirit: "You are compelled to be free to do things your own way. You are an independent thinker. You like to be free to be your own boss, to come and go as you please, and to dance to the beat of your own drum. Because you like to be free from constraints and regulations, you are naturally self-directed. You need to be in an environment where you can be independent."

I'm a Celebrity: "You have a natural ease under the spotlight. You thrive in public situations. Because you love the response, you are comfortable in front of an audience. You can achieve a high level of notoriety. You have an innate ability to stand head and shoulders above the rest. You desire to see your name in lights. People love being around you because you are effervescent, exuberant, and spontaneous."

I'm a Team Player: "You are compelled to have a sense of belonging, a sense of intimacy, a connection with others. You enjoy the camaraderie and interaction that a team environment offers. You enjoy being united with others in your accomplishments. You are appreciated as a team player because of your loyalty and commitment."

I'm a Conqueror: "As a conqueror, you are compelled to be the best, the ultimate, the winner. You are VERY competitive. You are conscious of others' efforts and accomplishments, as you use them as reference points to be better, stronger, and faster. Because you do not like the status quo, you are always striving to surpass your personal best or that of the competition. You are frustrated by second place."

I'm an Organizer: "You are not intimidated by chaos. You think structurally, from your every thought to your sock drawer, to establish a sense of symmetry in your life. You are compelled to restore order to a situation, relationship, or project. You can take a complicated problem and naturally simplify it. You are great in a pinch. When things get chaotic and people around you are under stress from the chaos, you have an easy, steady-state response to those stressors. You instinctively find ways to bring calm and order."

I'm a Motivator: "You are hands-on and physically engage in your environment in order to achieve your agenda. You have the ability to physically execute a task, and to influence others to accomplish the task for you."

I'm Synergistic: "You process information in community, through the exchange of ideas. You love to brainstorm/synergize with others. You want a sense of team. Your team needs to be your coach, your assistant, and your sphere of influence—not your colleagues."

I'm Kinesthetic: "You learn by doing, by observing interesting people or even from your own mistakes (the school of life, hard knocks). Your confidence and competence comes when you can have something go through your hands. You love to engage the world around you in an experiential way. This brings vitality to your life and the lives of those around you."

I'm Aesthetic: "You are motivated by the expression of an idea, the nuance, the particular. You tend to evaluate progress and communication on the basis of style and symbolic realities. What matters to you is words, the intangible, heartfelt, poetic reality. Your motto is, 'Show me that you care by what you say and how you say it.' You need to be seen, acknowledged, and validated with meaningful words."

I'm Gregarious: "You revive around people. Without a lot of people interaction, you can become depressed. It is important that your work and play involve a lot of interaction with others. You value time spent with others. You are motivated by your significant relationships, parties, and social gatherings."

I'm Perpetual: "You do not naturally 'see time'; rather, you see 'events in time,' moving in a perpetual motion from one event to the next. This makes you far more tenacious than others to not give up, to keep going. However, natural breakpoints do not occur for you (such as eating regularly or stopping to celebrate finished achievements), which can lead to physical or emotional burnout." (Oh my God, is this ever true!)

I Execute and Finalize: "Your natural strength is in developing and finishing projects. When given a task, plan, or goal, you like to 'take the ball and run with it' and carry out the task until completion. However, you need external pressure points to get started. You like to carry a project to completion, to finish things, to get things done. It's important to you that you personally finish what you start."

I'm Rapid-Meticulous: "You have an extraordinary, painstaking attention to detail, yet you hate to be bogged down by details. You like to cover a lot of ground quickly. You can gift others with thoroughness and raising the standard of excellence while propelling others to action. You hate to make mistakes because of your high standards."

Who R U?

I'm Spectrum-Focused: "You have a balanced focus on life. You are able to process the events presently occurring and relate them to your future. You have 20/20 vision. You can see both the big picture and the ABCs needed to get there. You look for balance."

Anyway, I put this profile aside for a long time and simply thought, "Well, that's interesting." But it didn't necessarily mean that much to my life until I found my career calling, some 15 years later. It was then that everything kind of clicked into place. I went back to look at this book, and suddenly all of my attributes became assets. It ultimately stood as a guide for my future.

29 BLACK BUTTERFLY

IN 2013, EVERYTHING WAS CHANGING in my life, and I was miserable. I'd finally split from my husband after 16 years of a union that sucked the life out of me and had taken up with a new man. I had a newborn at home. I'd fallen into a depression and was living paycheck to paycheck. I'd been evicted from my townhome. I was residing in a new state (Texas) with no family or friends around. I'd been working at a call center doing telemarketing, selling people university directories for two years, a dead-end job. I was basically just flailing.

I remember going over and over again in my mind how I needed to find my sparkle again, my happy place. But how would I do it? At 42 years old, what could I do outside of music that was fun and that would get me out of that freaking office and in front of people again?

And then it happened. I was on Instagram one day when I saw a woman named Dana Barish in her boat on the water saying, "Heeeeey! I'm in my mobile office. What are you waiting for? This could be *you*. . . ."

Twenty years before, Dana was my broke fitness instructor, and I was a struggling, starving artist. Now, she was a consultant for this company called Pure Romance that sold bedroom toys and intimacy products to women during at-home parties. I'd never heard of these guys, much less been to one of their parties. But I had nothing to lose, so I checked out her Facebook page and reached out to Dana to discover what this thing was all about.

"This is a real business that can turn your life around, Angie," Dana assured me. "Take a chance on it. Why not?" We got caught up discussing our pasts. She too had gone through a divorce, and after listening to HER story, I really believed this was something that would help me get my mojo back.

"What do I need to do?" I asked.

Dana told me to go to her website right that minute and purchase a business starter kit for $189, plus tax and shipping.

What? Well, I needed this, but I was so damned broke I couldn't even pay attention. I told her that I needed to transfer some money and that I would call her back. I went to my son DJ, who at the time was working part time at Six Flags amusement park, and I asked if I could borrow the money from him.

I mean, what was he doing with his money, anyway? I was paying for everything he needed. He said the only thing he could say, right? Yes! I remember telling him that if he invested in me that we would be rich one day, and I would pay him back with interest.

So, I called Dana back, went on the site, and ordered the kit. I was taking Dana's word that this was a good idea. But there I was, seeing all these lubricants with names like Pure Pleasure, Just Like Me, Great Head, and Like a Virgin—and a women's shaving cream called Coochy! I was nervous. I didn't have experience with any of these things, and in fact I had no idea what

I was supposed to do with them. Would I be like the Avon or Mary Kay lady, except toting around a bunch of dildos?

I didn't want to offend God. I was trying to get my life back on track and make up for the mistakes I had made, but I was questioning if this was the right way to go about it. I didn't really get a lot of direction from Dana, who admittedly didn't have an onboarding system for her people. She didn't hold your hand. This was someone who was incredibly successful and had a team of over 5,000 women.

Still, I reached out and asked her, "Okay, what do I do now?"

"One of my girls is doing a party near you next Thursday night," she said. "Go shadow her."

Going in, I was concerned and didn't want to bust Hell wide open. (LOL) It's not even like I'm a conservative person, but the whole thing made me more than a little apprehensive. I had no idea what went on at these parties.

Instead of walking into what I imagined might have been the Best Little Whorehouse in Texas, I spent the evening with some fun girls who were super nice to me—and I had a blast. It was like girls' night. It was just what women already do when they get together, but with some organized games and a little selling mixed in. We laughed. We talked about relationships. We discussed sex. We chatted about life in general. I had the greatest time.

I was like, "*This* is the gig? I'm going to get paid to do *this*? To just have fun and talk to people and sell a few things? Count me in!"

That said, I wasn't very disciplined. My life had been kind of in a shambles, and I didn't turn it around overnight. Even at 42, I'd never had a career that I'd stuck with for any genuine length of time.

Things really changed for me after I went to the Pure Romance World Conference in March 2016 in Orlando. I saw all of these women taking home awards and being honored and getting these big old checks, and I said to myself, "I'm going to really figure this thing out and walk that stage next year."

And I did. I got myself fired from my call center job on purpose and lived off unemployment so I could build this up and do it full time. For the first time in my life, I would begin making six figures as Senior Executive Director and become the first African American woman to hold the title. I also earned a seat on the Board of Directors.

As if that weren't exciting enough, I quickly found out that less than 1% of women in the business even hold this title! What an achievement, and something I made happen in 2020 in the midst of a freaking pandemic, too. Just wow! I was and remain so proud of myself.

The biggest change for me came when Chris Cicchinelli, the company's genius of a President and CEO, put me into his Future Leader Program during my very first year with them. That provided me with a structured way of doing things and an outcome I never imagined I could get. What it offered me was accountability. It turned out this was what I needed more than anything.

At the same time, I quickly forgot about any moral issue in selling intimacy products. What I learned from Patty Brisben, founder of Pure Romance and Cicchinelli's mother, was that I wasn't promoting promiscuity but just the opposite. I was helping to keep married people together and single people safe. I was simply helping singles and couples improve their relationships—even if that relationship was with themselves.

I was giving my daughters the proper education about their sexual health as well, which I now know is extremely important. The only pushback on me came from my mother. She would tell people, "Oh my God, now Angie is selling sex toys! What is she doing?"

But I was having a conversation with her one day where she was sharing some of the intimate details of her life, and I said, "Mom, don't you know this is what I teach women about every day?" She allowed me to educate her and wound up replying, "Wow, if I'd have known all this stuff, I'd have gotten a vibrator a long time ago." Of course, I hooked her up. I'm out here saving the world one vagina at a time, my mom's included! LOL!

Surprisingly, despite coming from the very judgmental gospel and Christian music industry, I never got any pushback from them. They supported it and were even intrigued by it.

The biggest challenge for me was learning the work/life balance. There were times when I was up all night either closing out a party or planning things for my team, The Zealous Zebras. I literally didn't sleep, because I'm a resolution junkie. Customer service is my #1 priority, so there were nights I would go through all my order forms and send out follow-up messages to everybody. I like to strike while the iron is hot and reach out to my team to give them follow-up information. I love what I do, and I live, eat, sleep, and breathe Pure Romance. So, avoiding staying a workaholic and being present when I was with my family, that was and still is the hardest thing for me.

For somebody like me who gets bored far too easily, this job became the cure-all. The independence, the money, the ability to enhance people's intimate relationships, it's all been amazing. In my past jobs, I always gave 110 percent, which came with some nice rewards, but nothing compared to what I get from Pure Romance.

In my previous jobs, I lacked passion. Nothing kept my interest very long. That's been impossible for me at this company. You can't get bored. There are always new products. There are always new people. You can always change a party up and do a new game. I needed something that I couldn't get sick of, and it took until I was in my 40's to find it. But I did.

As far as any stigma in selling products that enhance genital stimulation, sex, and masturbation, let me just offer a single word: None. Not for me. Never been an issue. There might have been instead a little concern that, being a minority myself, most of my parties in the beginning were with minority women who didn't have the education in sex and sexual health.

Whereas they might spend $200 on a pair of Jordans or $600 on a designer handbag, they weren't going to fork over $200 on a vibrator, because they didn't see the value in it. But as my mentor Chris told me in my first

Future Leader class, "It's not about race. It's about education." That has turned out to be true. For my minority clients, I'm educating, and they're growing with me. My client base is now very diverse. They love and take care of me, and I love and take care of them.

I've been blessed to have the opportunity to set an example for my fellow consultants of color. Not to toot my own horn, but there was a shifting that took place with what I brought to Pure Romance. That is not my own observation but that of many others.

In fact, I received another message today from a sister consultant thanking me for my example, which allowed her to see success in her future. It's been said that seeing someone who looks like them accomplish so much and receive so many accolades alters the dynamic in their mind. For that reason, I've been careful to make myself very, very visible. Fortunately, I'm used to it because of my experience in the entertainment industry.

My sales team and I created a culture where people can see that this business isn't just about white women. This is a "you do, you get" business. So, we've worked to elevate each other rather than tear one another down. In my experience, there's been a lot of jealousy within my own race, and the result is to try to crush each other to bring ourselves up. I worked to make sure that didn't happen at Pure Romance, as did Chris, Patty, and the entire corporate staff.

I admit that I was a little hesitant at first to work closely with my fellow black and brown women, due to the resentment and betrayal I had endured in the past. Unfortunately, there has been a history where people were afraid to share too many of their secrets (or any at all) due to the fear you would outshine them. That had been the story of my life, and the last thing I wanted was to be associated with a mean group of women stabbing each other in the back.

I changed my perspective when I started forming beautiful relationships with ladies like Cynthia Cosby, an Advanced Director with Pure Romance. I also saw that the people overseeing things at Pure Romance, headed by Chris, did nothing to hinder our growth in the company and only encouraged it. This was a true sisterhood in every sense of the word. That made all the difference.

As I mentioned, I've been doing this only five years as you read these words, and I hit retail sales of six figures in income by my third year. It went up a little bit in 2018 and 2019, and then exploded in 2020 during the pandemic, when we were ALL shocked to see the giant level of our growth. But quite honestly, my focus is on my team and building leaders rather than on my personal increases.

Pure Romance is a multi-level marketing company, which means I bring new people in all the time. It isn't that I have to. I choose to. The more women who become consultants on my team, the more I earn. That's the beauty of our compensation plan.

With 2020 came the COVID-19 pandemic, right? Well now, imagine this: You're in a job that depends 100 percent on being with people in parties in a home. Take away the ability of people to congregate in the same space. What do you do? We were all concerned at first that this was going to be the end of our livelihoods. I mean, how could we not?

None of us had any idea what the virus was going to mean for our business. I, for one, had no trouble pivoting away from in-home parties. Then we saw something like 250-plus percent growth throughout the springtime last year and into the summer, doing virtual parties over Zoom and Facebook.

But to be honest, Chris is such a phenomenal businessman and a great coach that once he started discussing it with us, I was never once fearful things weren't going to go our way. That's the truth. He was like, "Just in case we get shut down, I'm going to set things up so you guys have mini-warehouses, so you have inventory." That was very reassuring.

This business has definitely been changed by the pandemic for the long haul, no question—and unbelievably, in a positive way. I think that it's opened things up for us. What we learned during COVID ultimately gave us more opportunity and greater reach.

For example, I was able to hold a virtual party in 2020 with a group of sorority sisters in Bermuda. It was perfect for them. They had not seen each other in a long time, and they all managed to be in their own bedrooms or living rooms sipping a cocktail and ordering products over Zoom.

I feel like we as a company are coming out of this better than if the pandemic had never happened in the first place. It helps that I'm the kind of person who jumps off the cliff and figures out how I'm going to land on the way down.

The truth is that none of it would have been possible without Chris Cicchinelli's honesty, integrity, and business smarts. I still remember what he told us when everything was starting to roll during the pandemic: "Listen, ride this wave while you can, because things are going to level off. We know everybody's making crazy money now, but don't spend it, put it away, because this isn't going on forever."

Chris moved during the most uncertain time without fear. I mean, he was scared. You could tell he was apprehensive, but he reassured us that we would pivot and make this work and come out of this thing okay. And he was right.

I have met a lot of great leaders, both in the church and outside of it, in business, all over. But no one ever drew me to them like Chris has. He is just an authentic leader. I love the way he has our backs and takes care of the team like we're all family. He's helped me to get my life in order financially, in every which way. He's been a total and complete blessing for all of us.

I'm a strong woman. And while the things I've been through have damaged me in a lot of ways, this company—the sisterhood, the camaraderie, the leadership—empowered me in a way I never imagined. I feel like freaking superwoman, and nobody can touch me!

There have been women in my shopping room who were sexually abused, who were survivors like me. So many aspects of my journey prepared me to help other women who are going through stuff to get in touch with their sexuality in a healthy and dynamic way. I just happened to stumble into the perfect career.

That said, everything was not always rainbows and roses. There WERE a few bumps in the road at the beginning, even in my current fabulous position.

A few of the girls and I were working on strategies to sponsor more women into the business by doing live chats on Facebook. These were mini interviews, where we discussed how we got involved with Pure Romance, where we came from, like that. But somehow when I did it, I guess I stood out a little bit more than the others. One of the girls was really bothered by that, perceiving that I was hogging the spotlight.

My take was, "Aren't we *supposed* to be doing this—so we stand out more? But now you're telling me to shrink and you're angry with me?" It didn't feel like much of a team concept to me. Shortly thereafter, at a leadership retreat for the Diamond Divas (Dana's team), I got a chance to sit down with Dana—my sponsor—and she determined that I was "trapped in fear."

Now, I should say here that Dana is a shaman. She's very much into the stones and the crystals, she reads palms, all of that kind of "woo-woo" stuff. So, she had these Angel cards out, and that's where she revealed my coming from a place of fear.

What she had observed was extremely perceptive, because it fed into the idea that I've always, throughout my life, been pushed into a position of standing out, of shining, of leadership, because people gravitated toward

Who R U?

me. But it's made some people resent me in the process. *That's* my fear—that if I'm myself, people won't like me.

"Angie," Dana said to me, "pretty much everybody loves you. Corporate loves you. You're a leader in this organization."

"You know," I replied, "the fear is probably that I'm afraid as I climb the ladder, more people will reject me."

"Okay, Angie, I take it back: everybody's *not* going to like you," Dana shot back. "You think everybody likes Oprah? That isn't how things work. You don't even have to do anything wrong to anyone. Some people will just not like you because they don't like you. They'll be jealous. It's human nature. You can't do anything about it, so don't worry about it."

It was shortly thereafter that I concluded I didn't need to be a part of this other group that had kind of segregated itself off, which never felt good or right to me, anyway. I was simply trying to be helpful, a team player, but I felt so much hostility within it. I can't do chaos and negativity. It paralyzes me. So, I took myself away from that group and began to soar on my own. It taught me patience, perseverance, and courage.

One of the things I've learned about myself is that I get a lot of joy from mentoring and helping people become the best version of themselves. I lead this Elite Lifestyle Earners Program that I developed within my team, elevating women in whom I see a lot of potential to become leaders not only in Pure Romance but in life. It's the kind of thing I didn't even realize I needed until Chris put me into his Future Leader Program, so I took a page from his book and now dedicate lots of time and energy to the fortunate ladies who qualify for the program every quarter.

The program has really helped my team to grow tremendously, and to see these incredibly strong women flourish daily feeds my soul like you wouldn't believe. I'm excited and feel privileged to live my life in such a state of bliss.

There is also something to be said about growth, confidence, and fearlessness. I'm fortunate to possess all of those attributes in spades. I owe so much of it to Pure Romance.

The love affair that I have with the company I'm partnered with empowers me every single day. And empowering women, I have come to understand, is what I was put on this earth to do. It's my purpose.

30 PURPOSE

THIS IS WHERE I PUT on my motivational speaker hat for a minute and tell you how I finally got up the nerve to leave a dead-end marriage after 16 years. I ultimately made a decision to love myself. Women who are similarly trapped need to find out who they are and what their purpose is and make that their mission.

Remember, it's never too late to be who or what you might have been. There's so much freedom in finding your purpose in life, because once you do, you become laser-focused on it. I don't care what's happening around you, nothing is going to stop you from fulfilling it.

Once you adopt that mindset, you find your purpose, you believe in it, you have a passion for it, and you become so driven that it almost becomes like the air you breathe. You need it to survive. You just block out everything that's sucking the oxygen from you and attempting to take you off your focus.

My advice is to do everything in your power to remove negativity from around you. Get out of the vicious cycles of negative energy and people. That can be an especially difficult thing for those in the African American community, where family loyalty is a BIG thing, and people can feel imprisoned by their relatives who are toxic to their lives.

As I noted at the end of the last chapter, my purpose has always been to empower the women around me. I started to take that especially seriously when I stumbled onto Pure Romance. People need love, acceptance, and healing, and sometimes that healing can be as simple as saying these five words, "I'm so proud of you."

Therefore, I say them again, this time specifically to you who have accompanied me on this literary journey: "I'm so proud of you." You might be shocked to know (or maybe not) just how many people never hear that phrase. They don't hear it from their parents. They don't hear it from their friends. Too many of us are just so tied up in our own head and with our own thing that we never take a moment to give those around us that validation.

So, let me just tell you right here and right now that I'm so proud of you for reading my book to the very end—and I appreciate you. I believe that reading my autobiography means you love yourself enough to be willing to learn and grow from someone else's mistakes.

You are on the path to taking back everything that was ever stolen from you. Above all, I hope I have left you feeling supported, inspired, and empowered. The next time someone tries to bash you with your past mistakes or tries to label or judge you, I want you to hold your head up high and say these words: WHO R U?

ACKNOWLEDGEMENTS

No book like this can come together without the love, assistance, and guidance of so many people and forces. Mine is no exception.

First, I need to single out my parents. Thank you for the strength and the life lessons. We have been through so much, and yet we are still here. I forgive you for anything I may have felt you were responsible for that impacted me negatively. I believe in my heart that you would never intentionally cause harm or heartache toward me. I pray that you forgive me as well for those things I have done or said to you that were hurtful or disrespectful. I love you both with all my heart. Dad, thanks for being such an amazing entrepreneur. It has helped pave the way for my success. Mom, thanks for being an example of hard work and dedication. I pray that you find your happiness and peace, and that maybe one day we can learn to love each other without condition.

To my five children: I LOVE YOU DEEPLY and always will! You all have probably saved my life, and for that I am eternally grateful. I pray for our restoration daily and WILL see it come to pass.

To my sisters: Thank you for always loving me and being there for me, no matter what. We too have had our ups and downs, but without your nurturing nature, my elder sister, I don't know who I would be today. You have been the best sister-mom a girl could ever have. And to my younger sister, thanks for the fun. It does good like a medicine. I LOVE YOU BOTH TO LIFE!

To my FAVORITE Uncle Kirk: You too have been a constant in my life, and I appreciate you more than you could ever know. I tear up even as I write this. Your confidence in me, your praises toward me, your non-judgment of me has meant EVERYTHING to the success of me living life to the fullest. You are truly heaven-sent!

To Brie, my Ride or Die: Thanks for always having my back. Our friendship means more to me than words could ever convey. As we always say, *From the Wirt to the Dirt "ABLE" LOL* (wink).

To Hakim: Thank you for being the brother I never had and for supporting my dreams without question. You have never judged me and have always been there to catch me BEFORE I fell. Being called your sister is an honor. I love you!

To Justino, *a.k.a.* Angel: Thank you for your continued support by helping to hold our family together in the toughest of storms. Thank you for allowing me to work day and night on this project while taking care of our home, serving me breakfast in bed, dinner at night, and so much more. You always said that I was a touchdown type of chick and that we would rewrite our story—and we have. We are both much better individuals as a result of our

journey together. You have helped to make me stronger. God knew I would need it for the adventure that lay ahead, and so for that I am eternally grateful. Through thick and thin, we win! I will always love you.

To Jackie Hicks: Thanks so much for opening me up to a whole new world. It was your gift and your heart that helped make it possible for me to take the gospel industry by storm, along with many other opportunities beyond that. Thanks for the cornbread and sweet potato recipe, too—you are a real one! (JOHNSON!) (Smile.)

To Dana Barish: I'm *so* glad we met. You started out being instrumental in helping to transform my body, and then with a full-circle moment you led me on a path to help transform my mind. Thank you for the opportunity and continued support.

To my two Angels, Molly and MJ: I am eternally grateful for the love you showed me. You were instrumental in helping me to get here. If it were not for what you did that night (you know which one I'm talking about), this story likely would have ended very differently.

To Chris Cicchinelli: Thank you for being such an amazing mentor to me. I have met and worked with many people in business over the years, but no one has ever spoken to my heart and mind the way that you have. Who would have thought that, at 42 years old, I would meet you and my life would be changed forever? May God continue to bless you and your family forever and ever.

To Patty Brisben: Thank you for being FEARLESS and paving the way for women like me! I pray I have represented you well.

To Cynthia Cosby, my TEAM NO SLEEP sista: Thank you for always encouraging me and for the many meaningful gifts that will always help to reassure me of WHO I AM! Have Paris ready for me upon my return (smile).

To the Zealous Zebras, my AMAZING team of women: I am humbled every day by how you ladies allow me to lead you on your journey to become the best version of yourselves. Thank you for trusting me. My heart is always FOR you.

To my clients and the ENTIRE Pure Romance Family: You have helped to heal wounds that were caused by many people over the years. That abuse kept me trapped and unable to grow and reach my full potential. Your unconditional love, respect, and adoration has accomplished what I once thought was impossible. I pray that you get to experience what this feels like if you have not already. It is the most magical feeling, and YOU played a huge part in that.

To Debbie S: I am grateful for the woman you helped me to become by nurturing me in ways that a mother always should. I wish things could have been different. Although you broke my heart when you abandoned me, I know you had no choice, and so I forgive you.

To the Snipes family: THANK YOU FOR BEING OUR SHELTER IN THE TIME OF STORM.

SHOUT OUT TO THE "WHO R U?" GLAM SQUAD! Makeup Artist Brianna Meshack, Custom Wig Designer Tangela Tenae, Photographer Darnell Porter, Videographer/Photographer Robert Woodard III (ConvilleKreations), and Wardrobe Stylist Jay Jones. Thank you for all you did!

To Ray Richmond: I don't believe that anything is by chance. I'm grateful for the opportunity to have connected with you. You have helped to fulfill a lifelong dream, something I knew was preordained, to come to fruition. You have made this process so light and entertaining. I look forward to celebrating this future *New York Times Bestseller* with you over dinner. YOUR TREAT! LOL! Just know I wish you much continued success.

Finally, to my GOD: Your grace has kept me and been sufficient. Thank you for forgiving me time and time again, for choosing me to serve your purpose, and for never taking your Holy Spirit away.

ABOUT THE AUTHOR

Angelia Robinson is a successful singer-turned-entrepreneur who finally found her calling with Pure Romance, the world's largest woman-to-woman direct seller of relationship enhancement products. She began with the company in 2015 as a sales consultant, working her way up to Senior Executive Director and a member of the company's Board of Directors.

A resident of Ft. Worth, Texas, and a mother of five, Angelia is looking to inspire and empower as many women as she can through her work, through her book, and by example through her purpose-driven life. If you like *Who R U?*, she is hoping you will take a moment to give it a review on *Amazon*, on *Goodreads*, on *Barnes & Noble*, or through any of the online sites that sell and critique books.

Angie would also love to hear back from you directly at *whorubio@gmail.com*, where she promises to answer every email.

Want to get connected with Angelia? Be sure to follow or friend her on social media. She can be reached via:

Facebook: angeliarobinson
Twitter: @partygirlangeli
Instagram: angeliaspureromance
Website: angeliarobinson.com
Snapchat: angeliaspr
TikTok: @angeliarobinson3

CPSIA information can be obtained
at www.ICGtesting.com
Printed in the USA
LVHW100602300321
682902LV00002B/3